Helping Ourselves

A Guide to Traditional Chinese Food Energetics

Meridian Press
Totnes, England

ACKNOWLEDGEMENTS

I am grateful for lengthy consultations with Dr. Yifang Zhang, acupuncturist, herbalist and lecturer at Nanjing University and to the advice and encouragement of John and Angela Hicks, directors of The College of Integrated Chinese Medicine. Thankyou also to Katheryn Trenshaw for her loving support during the making of this book.

First published in Great Britain by Meridian Press 1994
Reprinted 1995, 1997, 2000, 2003
Second Edition 2005, Reprinted 2008, 2012, 2014
© Daverick Leggett

Cover, illustrations and design by Katheryn Trenshaw
Illustrations © Katheryn Trenshaw 1994
ISBN 978 0 9524640 0 4

Published by

Meridian Press

P.O. Box 3
Totnes
Devon TQ9 5WJ
England

Tel & Fax: 0845 456 1852
post@meridianpress.net
www.meridianpress.net

The Green Pages Pledge

Books are made from trees. At all stages of the production of this book care has been taken to minimise the environmental impact: recycled and scrap paper was used for all stages up to publication; the book has been printed on recycled paper; packaging has made full use of reclaimed and recycled material; all waste paper has been re-used or recycled. In addition, the author makes a commitment that a percentage of the profits from the sale of this book will be used to plant new trees at least equivalent to the total paper use involved in all aspects of its publication and distribution.

CONTENTS

INTRODUCTION

This manual grew out of a desire to offer my clients ways of continuing in daily life the work they do with me in Shiatsu and Qigong. It is intended both as a learning resource for students and clients of Traditional Chinese Medicine and as a reference manual for practitioners. My hope is that it will become a positive force for wellbeing in the lives of all who use it.

To the practitioner *Helping Ourselves* offers a comprehensive reference manual to turn to time and again when offering guidance to clients. It is designed in an accessible format for direct clinical use. The structure reflects the logical progression of building the diagnostic picture. When designing the manual I conceived it as something I could pass onto my clients to empower them in their own healing.

To the student it offers a way into Traditional Chinese Medicine that is tangible and directly applicable. In my own teaching experience I have found the exploration of food energetics to be one of the easiest ways to develop an understanding of Traditional Chinese Medicine. It also provides a great excuse for feasting together!

To the client of oriental acupuncture, bodywork or herbalism *Helping Ourselves* is a manual to take home which offers a way of carrying treatment into daily life. It provides the self-help tool which so many clients ask for, a way of becoming more active in our own healing process.

The information in this manual is derived from the accumulated wisdom of several thousand years of Chinese Medicine. It does not offer a quick-fix or a guilt-trip or encourage sudden dietary revolution. It is offered as an opportunity to explore, to play, to learn. It is a tool for us to use to engage more consciously and skilfully with life. Please take it in this spirit and don't use it as a way of making yourself miserable. If I could offer only one piece of advice, it would be this: enjoy your food, and don't worry.

Five years and a baby after writing *Helping Ourselves* I wrote its sequel, *Recipes for Self-Healing*. Recipes explores in greater depth the whole issue of nourishment and offers a hundred recipes, rooted in western cuisine, that apply the wisdoms of Chinese medicine in the western kitchen. Together with the wallcharts, *The Energetics of Food* and *The Energetics of Herbs*, these four works may be considered a complete set. I encourage you to buy them all (of course). Please refer to the back pages for details of how to do this.

NOTE
Eating disorders and severe medical conditions

Eating disorders sometimes derive from severe childhood trauma such as emotional, physical or sexual abuse. Although the principles of Traditional Chinese Medicine are universally valid, a purely dietary approach is rarely helpful. Those readers who identify themselves as having eating disorders such as anorexia or bulimia may wish to consider working more directly with the underlying emotional cause and are not advised to use this manual without skilled help.

Similarly, those with severe medical conditions are advised not to use this manual without also consulting their health professional. Helping Ourselves is intended as a supplement to, not a substitute for, skilled professional guidance.

PART ONE

How To Use This Book

INTRODUCING THE SPLEEN

We begin our journey by looking at the central Organ of digestion in Chinese medicine: the Spleen.

As infants we learn to adapt to whatever environment we are born into. This remarkable and beautiful skill, the ability to adapt to our environment and get our needs met, is one of the functions of the Spleen in Traditional Chinese Medicine. We can think of the Spleen as the Organ of adaptation.

This may seem a strange definition to a Westerner, for whom an organ is a specific location in the body where certain tasks are performed but in the language of Traditional Chinese Medicine an Organ is a set of functions which are expressed in various ways throughout the bodymind. The functions of the Spleen are adaptation, nourishment and support (the set of skills through which we get our needs met). As we shall see, these functions are expressed at a physiological, anatomical, mental, emotional and spiritual level.

At the physiological level the Spleen is expressed as the digestive system, the means by which we meet our nutritional needs. Digestion is the process of converting food into usable substances within our bodies and sending them to where they are needed. The Spleen adapts food to nourish and support our system. This process is called 'transformation and transportation'. The stronger our Spleen function is, the better we are able to extract nourishment from any food to support our body's needs.

When we eat, the question is not so much whether a particular food is good for us but rather how strong and skilled our Spleen is at extracting the nourishment from it. The first step towards eating well may not involve changing our diet at all but rather strengthening and maintaining our Spleen. We shall see how to do this later.

The Spleen's physical manifestation as the digestive process is expressed at the mental level as the thinking process. The Spleen governs our ability to study and concentrate, to process information. Although it may not seem so at first glance, the thinking and digestive processes are very similar. When we read a book (this one for example) we have to adapt words (food) into sense (nutritional substances) and then store them or put them to use.

We recognise this connection when we say "This book is hard to digest" or "I need time to chew this over" or "There's food for thought". The Spleen's function is to adapt both food and information into something we can use.

There are other ways we can observe the connection between eating and thinking. Overeating, for example, may make the mind sluggish; too much studying often produces cravings for sweet foods; too much worrying (a knotted form of thinking) can easily knot the digestive system. Our powers of concentration and digestion are related and each will influence the other.

At the emotional level the Spleen is expressed through our ability to meet our needs, to obtain and give emotional nourishment and support. When our needs are met we feel nourished and supported, comfortable and secure in our lives. Often we confuse emotional and nutritional needs, eating when in fact we need comfort or perhaps using foods to suppress feelings such as frustration or desire. From the moment we first suck on our mother's breast the link between food and comfort is established.

So our ability to find and receive emotional nourishment is intimately linked with our digestive system. As we wean ourselves from mother and, later, from our parental home, we develop an internal mother and an internal home which we carry round inside ourselves as a constant source of nourishment and support. The internal mother and home is another description of the role of the Spleen.

It is easy to see how the quality of our early nurturing, both physical and emotional, deeply influences our ability to develop this internal sense of self-support. Our belief that we completely deserve nourishment and our trust that there will always be enough nourishment available are thus key elements in developing a strong Spleen.

We have looked at the physiological expression of Spleen as the digestive process. Anatomically the Spleen is expressed through the fascia and soft tissue. The fascia are a continuous network of moist membranous wrappings that connect the whole body and hold everything comfortably in place. Without the fascia our bodies would have no tone and we would collapse in a saggy heap. The fascia express the Spleen's function of support and containment.

When our fascia are relaxed and without constriction, all the subtle and larger movements of the body are smooth and easy. Our limbs have a full range of supple movement and our organs are supported in their functions. Our fascia contort and tense, or relax and spread, in direct response to our deepest held emotions. When the fascia are free we feel toned and comfortable in our bodies, supported from inside. We are 'at home' in our bodies, comfortable with who we are in the flesh. Being at home in our bodies is an expression of strong Spleen energy.

The stronger our Spleen is, the better we are able to absorb and put to use the food that we eat. So how can we strengthen and maintain our Spleen? This question can be answered at several levels.

Physically the Spleen likes to stretch. Stretching eases out constrictions in the soft tissue and brings relaxed tone to our limbs and organs. All exercise will help the Spleen provided it is balanced by stretching and relaxation. Massage will also help, releasing toxic build-up from our muscles and encouraging us to soften deep inside ourselves. The Spleen likes nourishing physical contact.

Mentally it is helpful to train the mind just as it is helpful to stretch and exercise our bodies. On the other hand, overuse of our mental powers (i.e. in prolonged periods of study, or in tasks that involve hours of sitting and processing information, or even habitual brooding on our problems) can weaken our Spleen. It is important to balance mental work with physical exercise and fresh air.

Emotionally we can explore and honour our needs. For some this may simply mean being kinder to ourselves, treating ourselves well; for some it may mean joining a supportive group; for some it may mean finding ways to deeper fulfilment in our relationships.

Finally, within oriental medicine, each Organ belongs to a particular element. The Spleen belongs to the Earth element, the earth being our provider of nourishment and support, our true mother. It is through our connectedness to the Earth and to the Divine Mother that the Spleen finds its spiritual expression. We can do a great deal to support our Spleen by attending to our relationship with the Earth.

Attending to our relationship with the Earth may mean becoming more grounded, simply giving more attention to the ground beneath our feet both physically and metaphorically. When done with awareness, all activity which connects us more deeply with the Earth, whether it be gardening, working with clay or simply being outdoors with the soil, the plants, the seasons, all these can help ground us in our bodies and in the natural environment. In these ways too we can support and strengthen our Spleen.

It is important to keep this wide perspective on the Spleen when considering dietary issues. We can strengthen our Spleen by working at any of the above levels and change at one level will resonate throughout the Spleen's whole sphere of influence. With this wide perspective in mind, we can go on to look at the dietary approach to supporting our Spleen.

EATING WELL
SOME GENERAL CONSIDERATIONS

Now that we have set the Spleen in its broader context let us look more specifically at how to assist the Spleen in its digestive function. After many years of working with my own and my clients' dietary needs, I have come to the conclusion that the following general guidelines are more valuable even than the detailed understanding of food to be found later in this book. The first of these is joy.

Joy. Enjoying our food is part of opening to being fully nourished by what we eat. If we are happy when we eat and happy in our relationship with food, then our bodies will literally accept the food more effectively into our system. Often it is more important for us to heal our relationship with food than it is to change what we eat.

Positive Attitude. Often we develop beliefs about 'good' or 'bad' foods. Some foods are 'good for us' even if we don't enjoy them. Other foods are 'bad for us' and we eat them guiltily or avoid them resentfully. Although common sense tells us that there is some truth in these labels, our attitude to the food we eat will instruct our Spleen what to do with it. So whatever we eat, once we have made a choice it is better to accept the food lovingly, to welcome the food as wholeheartedly as we can. In this way we will get the most out of all foods.

Relaxation. The Chinese believe that it is better not to mix food and work. Our digestion works best when we are focused on our enjoyment of the meal, not distracted or troubled by other influences. So it is better to make mealtime a relaxed occasion when we are not trying to read, watch television, do business etc.

It is helpful to take a little time to relax our posture too, perhaps take a few quiet breaths before eating. Crossing our legs, sitting twisted or hunched will compress our digestive organs and hinder the passage of food through our body.

Chew well. There is a saying that "The stomach has no teeth". Well chewed food lessens the work our digestive organs have to do and increases the efficient extraction of nutrients. Chewing also warms chilled food.

Stop just before you are full. In a culture of plenty this can sometimes be difficult. If we overeat at any one meal, we create stagnation, a temporary queue of food waiting to be processed. As a result we feel tired while our energy is occupied digesting the excess food. If this is a habit, our Spleen becomes over-strained and may produce Mucus or Heat (see later sections).

Don't flood the Spleen. The Spleen does not like too much fluid with a meal. A little warm fluid with a meal is helpful, but too much dilutes the Spleen's action and weakens digestion: a teacupful is generally sufficient. Most fluid is best consumed between meals.

Don't chill the Spleen. Too much raw or chilled food or fluid will also weaken the Spleen. The digestive process needs warmth. This is expressed in oriental medicine as the Digestive Fire. Prolonged or excessive use of chilled or raw food will eventually severely weaken the Digestive Fire, leading to collapse of the Spleen function.

Eat the main meal early. When we eat late at night our system is naturally slowing down and the food sits around for longer in the digestive tubes. This creates Stagnation and, in the body's attempt to burn off the food, Heat is created and the Yin of the Stomach will be damaged. (See later sections for explanation of terms.)

Choose foods with strong lifeforce. It is helpful to include as much locally grown food and organic quality food in our diets as possible. In both cases the lifeforce is more strongly preserved. For the same reason it is helpful to eat plenty of fresh food. The lifeforce is also significantly damaged by microwave cooking, by excessive processing and by chemical preservation. The lifeforce is killed by irradiation and dangerously distorted by genetic manipulation.

Trust your body. Sometimes we crave our poison, but there is in each of us a deeper level of knowing. As we bring our awareness to our eating, we can begin to feel what our true needs are, what truly nourishes us. At first we may need to be guided by more analytical judgments, but as we listen inside we can begin to make choices from our bodies too. What makes us feel good at the deepest level is good for us. Over time we can cultivate this skill of separating our cravings and addictions from our deeper levels of guidance.

EATING WELL
SOME SPECIFIC CONSIDERATIONS

Although the essence of oriental medicine is that each person eats according to their constitution, it is possible to set out some broad guidelines about what constitutes a healthy diet. There are two main considerations.

Establishing a broad and balanced base

A diet based mainly on grains and vegetables is central to most cultures. Grains and vegetables provide a central core of nourishment that is easy on the digestion, a foundation for our health. If we divide food into three main categories, the following proportions are recommended.

Vegetables and Fruits	40-60%
Grains	20-40%
Beans, Dairy, Meat, Nuts	10-20%

It is also wise to eat widely and as often as possible to eat foods that are in season.

Making food easy to digest

The second consideration is how we prepare food. The process of digestion involves breaking food down into a warm soup in the Stomach. It is then ready to be transformed. The Spleen extracts the essences (or flavours) from this soup, turns them into usable substances then sends them to where they are needed. The cooking method most resembling the Stomach's action is the preparation of soups and stews. This soupy mixture is already warmed and broken down for the Spleen to act upon. Soups and stews are therefore the most Spleen-supportive meals.

This does not mean that we should limit our diet to soups and stews! However, the weaker our Spleen is, the more these methods will be useful to us. They are less work for our digestive system and nutrients are more easily absorbed. The Spleen has to work hardest when food is very rich (like fatty meat), raw or chilled. So to support our Spleen we need to eat only moderate amounts of rich foods, chew all food well (especially raw food) and avoid too much chilled food. Raw food is easier to digest the more finely it is chopped or grated and meat is easier to digest when broken down in soups or casseroles.

Finally, the moderate use of warm and pungent spices with cooked food will support the digestive process as will the consumption of small amounts of pickled vegetables after a meal.

Now that we have established some general guidelines we can look more specifically at the energetic properties of food.

HOW FOOD IS DESCRIBED IN TRADITIONAL CHINESE MEDICINE

In the West, food is described as containing certain amounts of protein, fat, minerals, vitamins and so on. This information is obtained in a laboratory by analysing foods, separating them into their basic ingredients. The nutritional value of a food is a statement of the sum total of its chemical ingredients before they enter the body.

In the East, food is described as possessing certain qualities such as a warming or cooling nature, possessing certain flavours or acting on our body in a certain way. This information is obtained by observing the behaviour of the body after a food has been consumed. The nutritional value of a food is stated as a set of energetic properties which describe the actions a food has on the human body.

The single most important category in oriental medicine is the energetic temperature of a food.

The Temperatures of Food

The temperatures of individual foods are listed in the charts towards the end of this book. According to oriental medicine a food may be either Hot, Warm, Neutral, Cool or Cold. Oats, Chicken and Onions, for example, are warming; Barley, Rabbit and Lettuce are cooling. This is not a measure of how hot or cold a food is to the taste. The temperature of a food is a measure of its effect on the body after digestion. Simply, does it warm us up or cool us down?

Cooling foods tend to direct energy inwards and downwards, cooling the upper and outer parts of the body first. Warming foods move energy upwards and outwards from the core, warming us from the inside out. Very hot foods such as Chilli Peppers heat us up intensely then cool us down through sweating. Warmer foods speed us up, cooler foods slow us down.

A knowledge of the temperatures of foods is intrinsic to all traditional cooking. A warming curry is balanced by cooling cucumber and yoghourt; hot lamb is balanced by cooling mint sauce; root vegetable soups warm us in winter, salads cool us in summer. Often we will instinctively know the temperature of a food before we consult the chart.

There are no absolute rules that govern whether a food will be warming or cooling. However, the following general guidelines may help to assess a food not listed in this book:

- Plants which take longer to grow (root vegetables, ginger) tend to be warmer than fast-growing foods (lettuce, courgette).
- Foods with high water content tend to be more cooling (melon, cucumber, marrow).
- Dried foods tend to be more warming than their fresh counterparts.
- Chemically fertilised foods which are forced to grow quickly tend to be cooler than their naturally grown counterparts.
- Some chemicals added to foods may produce Heat reactions.

The temperature of food will also be influenced by the cooking or preparation method. The effects of the various methods are as follows:

- Raw — Cooling
- Steamed — Cooling/Neutral
- Boiled — Neutral
- Stewed — Warming
- Stir-fried — Warming
- Baked — More Warming
- Deep-fried — Heating
- Roasted — More Heating
- Grilled — More Heating
- Barbecued — Most Heating

Longer and slower methods will also produce more warming effects than quicker methods i.e. a stew will be more warming if it is cooked slowly than if it is cooked quickly.

Knowing the temperatures of foods helps us to balance the overall effect of a meal to suit our body's needs. Those with cold constitutions or conditions need to eat more warming diets and vice-versa.

The Flavours of Food

The flavour describes an essential quality inherent in a food. It describes a potential which is liberated by the alchemy of cooking and digestion. Each flavour arises from one elemental power and is said to enter a particular Organ. There are five main flavours:

The SALTY flavour belongs to the Water element and enters the Kidney
The SOUR flavour belongs to the Wood element and enters the Liver
The BITTER flavour belongs to the Fire element and enters the Heart
The SWEET flavour belongs to the Earth element and enters the Spleen
The PUNGENT flavour belongs to the Metal element and enters the Lung

People often ask "If I crave a certain food does that mean it's good for me?" The answer is yes, and no. When we are out of balance we develop a craving to correct that imbalance. So the Spleen, for example, craves sweetness when it is in trouble. This craving is accurate in the sense that it tells us that our Spleen is out of balance and the craving is a message that stimulates us to rebalance ourselves. The sweet flavour helps strengthen our Spleen.

However, partly due to the availability within our culture of highly saturated foods (with fat, sugar, salt etc.) we quickly give ourselves such a huge dose of the remedial flavour that we overwhelm the Organ and create the opposite effect.

Whereas a moderate quantity of one flavour benefits its related Organ, too much of that flavour will overwhelm and damage it. A little salt, for example, benefits the Kidney but too much will inhibit its action. The flavour of a food can be said to carry the action of a food to a particular Organ.

The flavour also tells us something about a food's action:

The Salty Flavour

The salty flavour moves inward and downward, drawing the action of a food towards the centre and root of the body. The salty flavour moistens, softens and detoxifies, counteracting the hardening of muscles and glands. It regulates the moisture balance in the body, stimulates digestive function and improves concentration.

A little saltiness supplements the quality of the Blood but in excess the salty flavour can congeal the Blood, stress the Heart and overtax the Kidney. Its moistening action is beneficial for Dryness, but saltiness should be restricted in conditions of Dampness

The Sour Flavour

The sour flavour stimulates contraction and absorption. It has a 'gathering' or astringent effect. It is therefore used for all 'leaking' and 'sagging' conditions involving loss of body fluids such as sweating, diarrhoea and haemorrhage. It counteracts the effects of fatty foods, prevents stagnation and benefits digestive absorption. The sour flavour specifically stimulates secretions from the gall-bladder and pancreas and despite the acid nature of most sour food the effect is actually to lower the acidity of the intestines.

Sour foods are blood activators and stagnation eliminators. They are generally cleansing and detoxifying, helping to tone our system but in excess may cause over-contraction and over-retention of moisture.

The Bitter Flavour

The bitter flavour "drains and dries" as it travels downwards through the body. It will improve appetite, stimulate digestion and draw out Dampness and Heat. It should be reduced in conditions of Cold, Dryness or Deficiency. The bitter flavour acts mostly on the heart but also benefits the upper respiratory tract, digestive system and Liver.

In excess the bitter flavour can deplete Qi and moisture.

The Sweet Flavour

The Sweet flavour is by far the most common and all foods contain a measure of sweetness. The sweet flavour harmonises all other flavours and forms the centre of our diet, mildly stimulating the circulation and nourishing us.

The sweet flavour may be divided into 'Full Sweet' and 'Empty Sweet'. Full Sweet includes most meat, legumes, nuts, dairy and starchy vegetables and is considered tonifying and strengthening. Empty Sweet includes most fruits and sweeteners and is considered more cleansing and cooling. The full sweet flavour is used to treat Deficiency. Sweet foods are also moistening and will benefit Dryness.

In excess the sweet flavour leads to the formation of Phlegm and often Heat and any excess of sweetness should be avoided in Damp conditions. Its over-use may also damage the Kidney, Spleen and bones.

The Pungent Flavour

The pungent flavour disperses stagnation and promotes the circulation of energy and blood, sending energy outwards and upwards. It stimulates digestion and helps break through Mucus.

Care must be taken when choosing the temperature of pungent foods. Some hot pungents are so extreme that they eventually cool the body via sweating. Warm pungents produce longer lasting warming effects and will benefit Cold conditions. Cool pungents can be used when Heat is present.

As Damp and Stagnant conditions frequently involve underlying Deficiency, the use of pungents often needs to be supported by a tonifying diet. In excess the pungent flavour will over-stimulate and exhaust Qi and Blood.

A balanced diet includes the use of all flavours, with the sweet flavour occupying a central position. A balance of flavours reduces overeating, increases satisfaction and ensures better absorption of nutrients. We can increase or decrease our intake of a particular flavour according to our needs.

The Routes and Actions of Foods

The flavour ascribes a food to a particular element. A food is also said to enter particular meridian pathways, directing its effect towards particular Organs. Walnuts , for example, enter the Kidney meridian and almonds enter the Lung.

Some foods also have a specific therapeutic action. A food may either tonify a particular bodily substance or function (Yin, Yang, Qi, Blood) or it may reduce the influence of a pathological condition (Qi Stagnation, Blood Stagnation, Dampness, Heat or Cold). Walnuts, for example, tonify Yang and almonds counteract Phlegm.

When we combine the meridian route with the therapeutic action of foods we get a specific description of its therapeutic effect. In the above examples we find that Almonds remove Phlegm from the Lung and walnuts tonify the Yang of the Kidney .

This knowledge helps us choose foods to include in our diet which are tailor-made for our personal energetic needs.

PUTTING THIS INFORMATION TO USE
"THE DIETARY TILT"

It is best for everyone to eat a varied diet that includes all temperatures and all flavours of food. Knowing our individual needs helps us to tilt our diet slightly in one direction. A cold person will tilt their diet slightly towards the warming side of neutral, a hot person slightly to the cooling side. A person whose Yin is deficient will tend to favour foods that tonify Yin and reduce over-stimulating and hot foods, and so on.

The more extreme our imbalance, the more strong the corrective tilt can be. However, it must be stressed that if we tilt too far for too long we can damage ourselves. For example, if a Yin Deficient person eats Yin tonics and cooling foods to the exclusion of all else, the effect will be to weaken the Yang and worsen the overall imbalance.

It cannot be stressed enough that dietary remedies need to be gentle. A tilt, a leaning in the desired direction sustained over a long period of time will be of far greater benefit than a 'binge'. Only in short-term acute conditions should we use strong dietary tilts.

HOW TO USE THIS BOOK
A STEP BY STEP GUIDE

Step One

The first step is to know our condition, our current energetic make-up. Part Four will help you get started but it is not the place of this book to offer a guide to self-diagnosis. This is best done with the help of a registered practitioner of Oriental Medicine (see the addresses at the end of this book). Once we have our current picture we can proceed to Step Two.

Step Two

Read and adopt the basic guidelines on pages 9-13. This is probably more important than the information contained in the pages that follow and for many people these general guidelines are sufficient to significantly enhance wellbeing. If more is needed we can proceed to Step Three.

Step Three

Our diagnosis will either be one of Deficiency or Excess, or sometimes a combination of both. Look up the relevant pages in Part Two and follow the guidelines.

Step Four

We use the chart to help select foods of the temperature and flavour that suit our energetic picture. We can favour these foods in our diet to achieve our dietary tilt. This does not mean the absolute exclusion of any food or flavour.

Step Five

Our diagnosis may refer specifically to one or more Organs. As a refinement of steps one to four we can choose foods that exactly match our diagnosis for regular inclusion in our diet. Small quantities consumed on a regular basis are more effective than large irregular doses.

n.b. It is important to recognise that our constitution may change, just as the circumstances of our lives may change. Having children or moving home, for example, can shift our energetic patterns. Over time we may develop new patterns and our diet needs to respond to this.

We can now look at some examples of how this works in practice.

Examples

a) Kidney Yin Deficiency

Step One. With the help of our practitioner of oriental medicine, we establish that our energetic picture is best described as Kidney Yin Deficiency.

Step Two. We adopt the basic guidelines on eating well.

Step Three. We look up Yin Deficiency and follow the general guidelines: we avoid stimulants and hot foods, reduce our use of the stronger pungent and bitter flavours, and take good rest; we favour sweet and cool foods, and make more use of sour and salty foods; we include Yin tonifying foods in our diet which are listed at the foot of the page.

Step Four. We use the food chart on a regular basis to ensure that the overall balance of flavours and temperatures is tilted in favour of Yin Deficiency.

Step Five. We use the chart to find foods which tonify Yin and have a specific action on the Kidney. So we find Asparagus, Oyster and Sesame Seed. We can include a small quantity of these foods regularly in our diet.

b) Spleen Qi Deficiency

Step One. With the help of our practitioner of oriental medicine, we establish that our energetic picture is best described as Spleen Qi Deficiency.

Step Two. We adopt the basic guidelines on eating well.

Step Three. We look up Qi Deficiency and follow the general guidelines: we work with breathing, postural alignment and physical exercise and examine our inner and outer environment; we favour fresh organically grown foods, especially foods with sweet and warm qualities; we include Qi tonifying foods which are listed at the foot of the page.

Step Four. We use the food chart on a regular basis to ensure that the overall balance of flavours and temperatures is tilted in favour of Qi Deficiency.

Step Five. We use the chart to find foods which tonify Qi and have a specific action on the Spleen. So we find Chicken, Oats and Sweet Potato amongst the foods which tonify Spleen Qi. We include a small amount of these foods regularly in our diets.

c) Phlegm in the Lung

Step One. With the help of our practitioner of oriental medicine, we establish that our energetic picture is best described as Phlegm in the Lung.

Step Two. We adopt the basic guidelines on eating well.

Step Three. We look up Phlegm and follow the general guidelines: we avoid congesting foods and over-eating, strengthen our Spleen and include Phlegm resolving foods which are listed at the foot of the page.

Step Four. We use the food chart on a regular basis to ensure that the overall balance of flavours and temperatures is tilted in favour of reducing Phlegm.

Step Five. We use the chart to find foods which resolve Phlegm and have a specific action on the Lung. So we find Onion, Pear and Radish amongst the foods which reslove Lung Phlegm. We include a small amount of these foods regularly in our diets.

PART TWO

Patterns of Disharmony: Deficiency and Excess

YIN DEFICIENCY

Yin, the water of the body, is both lubricant and fuel. When the Yin is strong all body processes are "well-oiled" and we have a good reserve of fine quality nutrients to build new tissue and repair and maintain our bodies. Both mentally and emotionally we feel that there is plenty of water in the well to draw from when needed.

When the Yin is depleted we have probably been running on empty for quite some time, overdoing it in some way. We may have been ill for a long time or perhaps we were born with a weak constitution. When the Yin becomes low then we begin to burn up, borrowing resources that we can't replenish. The lack of cooling lubricant may well make us overheat and dry up. We need time to replenish ourselves and rest is vital. We need patience too as this replenishing takes time.

Whereas the key for increasing and maintaining Yang is activity, the key for restoring and supporting our Yin is rest.

Supporting Our Yin Through Food

When our Yin is deficient we need to avoid foods which stimulate us to use up energy we don't really have and to avoid foods which will aggravate our tendency to overheat. We should therefore avoid stimulants such as coffee, alcohol and sugar and the overuse of the more heating and drying pungent spices that release energy from the body.

We need instead to build, the process of 'anabolism'. Yin tonifying foods combine deep and subtle nourishment with moistening and often cooling qualities. Yin tonics travel deeply into the body replenishing our core and soothing our overworked system. They include many deeply nutritious foods such as creatures and plants from the seabed; various meats, nuts, seeds and beans; and many moist, cooling fruits.

Dairy products also benefit the Yin. As with all rich foods they need to be used cautiously, especially if a tendency towards Dampness is already present. When building and restoring our Yin we must beware of over-accumulating moisture which may be difficult to transform.

We must also beware of over-cooling our system. So if we are Yin Deficient and feel cold we can use more warming methods of food preparation and avoid the coldest foods.

Yin tonics tend to be sweet and cool. To tonify Yin we favour sweet, sour and salty over bitter and pungent flavours. Foods which especially tonify Yin are listed below.

Apple	*Duck*	*Milk*	*Pork*	*Sweet Potato*
Asparagus	*Egg*	*Mulberry*	*Rabbit*	*Tofu*
Avocado	*Frog*	*Nettle*	*Royal Jelly*	*Tomato*
Banana	*Honey*	*Oyster*	*Seaweed*	*Watermelon*
Cheese	*Kidney bean*	*Pea*	*Sesame*	*Wheat*
Clam	*Lemon*	*Pear*	*Spelt*	*Yam*
Crab	*Malt*	*Pineapple*	*Spinach*	
Cuttlefish	*Mango*	*Pomegranate*	*String bean*	

YANG DEFICIENCY

Yang is the Fire of the body. All the processes of life require heat. Without heat life slows down and eventually stops altogether. Our Yang keeps us warm and provides heat for all the body's functions. If our Yang is low we cool down and our metabolism slows down. The moist Yin of the body cannot be transformed and may begin to accumulate. As a result we begin to underfunction and we may become cold and sluggish.

To build the Yang means to fan up the flames, to tend the fire within. We can support this process by keeping warm and keeping moving. Physical exercise will produce heat which increases the power of Yang. At an emotional level our Yang represents our passionate engagement with life. The more we actively partake in our lives, the more we build our Yang.

Supporting Our Yang Through Food

When our Yang is deficient we need to avoid taking too much cold food and liquid into our bodies as this puts out the Digestive Fire. Instead we need to favour foods and cooking methods that warm us up.

This means choosing red pepper over cucumber, or trout over crab, or cherry over banana. Many of the warm and pungent spices will supplement the digestive fire and encourage warm circulation in the body. A meal's warming quality will be increased by longer cooking methods, which also encourage heat to penetrate deeper into the body.

A word of caution: it is a mistake to think "the hotter the better". If we heat ourselves up so much that we sweat, then energy is lost and we begin to cool. This illustrates the rule that Yin and Yang convert into one another at their extremes. Building Yang is a gradual process that takes time and persistence.

Yang tonics tend to be sweet, pungent and warming. Foods which especially tonify Yang are listed below.

Anchovy	*Cinnamon bark*	*Ginger (dried)*	*Nutmeg*	*Shrimp*
Aniseed	*Clove*	*Goat*	*Pistachio*	*Star Anise*
Basil	*Dill seed*	*Kidney*	*Quinoa*	*Thyme*
Cardamom	*Fennel seed*	*Lamb*	*Rosemary*	*Trout*
Chestnut	*Fenugreek seed*	*Lobster*	*Sage*	*Venison*
Chive seed	*Garlic*	*Mutton*	*Savory*	*Walnut*

QI DEFICIENCY

We make Qi by combining food and air. Our ability to make Qi will depend partly on our physical constitution, partly on our lifestyle. In its simplest sense our Qi is our available energy. We need energy for all the body's activity: for movement, for digestion, for warding off illness, to get through the day.

When the Qi is weak, this means that we are underfunctioning in some way. How this shows itself will depend on our individual strengths and weaknesses. For some, a particular organ may lack the power to do its job well. For others, insufficient Qi may cause lethargy or the immune system may become weak.

We can increase our available energy through breathing, physical exercise and postural alignment. Conversely we can lower our available energy through shallow breathing, sedentary lifestyle and distorted posture. Fresh air is also important as a source of good quality Qi.

Qi levels may be reduced by environmental factors such as electromagnetic fields or geopathic stress. In some natural environments the quality of Qi is particularly high, which we often experience as a sense of uplift. Our core beliefs and mental attitudes will also help determine our Qi level, life-affirming and self-valuing beliefs helping to give us fuller access to our vitality.

Qi easily becomes stagnant when its circulation in the body is restricted by tension. So relaxation is a major key to the liberation and formation of Qi. Qi Stagnation is discussed on page 33.

Supporting our Qi through Food

To support and increase our Qi we need to eat foods which release energy steadily into our system over a long period of time. This quality is partly described in the West as complex carbohydrates which provide a sustained source of energy.

It is also important to eat foods whose Qi has been interfered with as little as possible by processing, transport or irradiation. So we need to include as much fresh, local organic food in our diet as possible. Microwave cooking will also significantly deplete the level of available Qi in food.

Foods which tonify Qi tend to be sweet and often warm. Some foods which especially tonify Qi are listed below.

Almond	*Fig*	*Microalgae*	*Quinoa*	*Tempeh*
Beef	*Ginseng*	*Milk*	*Rabbit*	*Tofu*
Carrot	*Goose*	*Millet*	*Rice*	*Trout*
Cherry	*Grape*	*Molasses*	*Royal Jelly*	*Venison*
Chicken	*Ham*	*Oats*	*Sage*	*Yam*
Chickpea	*Herring*	*Octopus*	*Sardine*	
Coconut	*Lentil*	*Pheasant*	*Sweet Potato*	
Date	*Licorice*	*Pigeon*	*Shiitake mushroom*	
Eel	*Longan*	*Pigeon egg*	*Squash*	
Egg	*Mackerel*	*Potato*	*Sturgeon*	

BLOOD DEFICIENCY

The quality of our Blood is a measure of the available nourishment circulating in our body. Blood nourishes our muscles, organs, brain, every part of us. Its quality depends on the quality of food we eat and our ability to absorb nourishment. In other words it depends on the strength of our Spleen.

As well as being the source of nourishment for bodily activity, the Blood is also said to house the Mind, to provide the physical root of our consciousness. Body and Mind are integrated in the Blood. The Blood enables our thoughts and emotions to be grounded in the body. Its quality helps keep body and mind together.

When our Blood is strong we tend to feel vigorous, well-nourished and full-bloodedly alive. When our Blood is weak, we may feel under-nourished and not fully in touch with who we are. We may experience separation, as if our Mind floats, loosening its anchor. At night the Mind may float so much that we cannot sleep.

Our ability to produce Blood is strengthened by maintaining a balance between rest and physical activity. Physical activity strengthens the Spleen's ability to convert food into Blood and helps the Heart circulate it around the body. Rest, especially in the early afternoon, enables the Liver to renew the Blood during the day.

Supporting Our Blood Through Food

Blood is very easily improved through diet. A diet rich in fresh vegetables is essential. In particular, dark green leafy vegetables and chlorophyll-rich foods are helpful, especially when combined with grains. Adequate protein is also necessary.

All meat and fish, many beans and several seafoods will strengthen the Blood. In severe cases of Blood depletion, animal organs may be helpful.

As all food forms the basis of Blood, we may simply say eat well and widely. The overuse of fatty foods, denatured foods and sweetened or salted foods will tend to weaken the Blood. Foods which especially tonify Blood are listed below.

Aduki bean	*Chicken egg*	*Kale*	*Mussel*	*Seaweed*
Apricot	*Cuttlefish*	*Kelp*	*Nettle*	*Spinach*
Beef	*Dandelion*	*Kidney bean*	*Octopus*	*Stout*
Beetroot	*Dang Gui*	*Leafy greens*	*Oxtail*	*Squid*
Black Soybean	*Date*	*Liver*	*Oyster*	*Sweet Rice*
Bone marrow	*Fig*	*Longan*	*Parsley*	*Tempeh*
Cherry	*Grape*	*Microalgae*	*Sardine*	*Watercress*

ESSENCE DEFICIENCY

Essence, or Jing, is closely related to the Kidneys where it is stored. Essence provides the physical basis for life itself, the rootstock which supports and conditions our growth and development. It is partly inherited from our parents, partly cultivated and stored through lifestyle, eating and drinking. Our Jing is considered to be a highly precious substance, which, like an inheritance, should not be squandered.

When Essence is strong the deep vitality of the body carries us through life. Children develop normally; adults are ensured of their fertility and age gracefully. Someone with strong Essence has a strong constitution, overcomes illness or injury easily and has good stamina. Essence is easily depleted through a combination of pushing our bodies too hard and failing to nourish through good food and adequate rest.

Supporting Our Essence Through Food

We can deplete our Essence through the over-use of stimulants and lack of adequate minerals. We can safeguard our Essence through rest and meditation and through eating a broadly nourishing diet. Meat and fish stock are helpful, algae and bee products are deeply nourishing and help can also be found from eggs, nuts and seeds which are dense in nutrients. Good quality milk, preferably raw, may sometimes help and mineral supplementation is often needed. In general, foods which nourish the Yin will also nourish Jing. A few foods are seen as being particularly nourishing to the Jing and are listed below.

Almond	*Kidney*	*Mussel*	*Royal Jelly*
Artichoke leaf	*Liver*	*Nettle*	*Seaweed*
Bone marrow	*Microalgae*	*Oyster*	*Sesame seed*
Chicken Egg	*Milk, raw*	*Pollen*	*Walnut*

DAMPNESS

Dampness comes from the failure to burn off or transform moisture in the body. It is nearly always associated with a weak Spleen, often with a weak Kidney and sometimes with a weak Lung. Dampness can lodge in a specific part of the body or affect us more generally. As the word suggests, Dampness can make us feel heavy and tired. It can make us swell up and it can obstruct our body's functioning.

Some people are more prone to Dampness than others. A tendency towards Dampness can be aggravated by living in damp conditions or by a sedentary lifestyle. It needs the transformative power of the body's Yang to stop it accumulating. Eating in ways which inhibit our Spleen function or which injure the Yang will increase our tendency towards Dampness.

Dampness may also be caused by pathogens lodged in the body which have not been properly expelled or by the use of suppressant drugs.

In this book Dampness is divided into three kinds.

Dampness

This describes a generalised condition of Dampness associated with weakness of the Spleen. It may manifest in such ways as tiredness/ache in the limbs, digestive weakness or muzzy head. How it manifests depends on our individual constitution.

Water

This describes a condition of edema where Dampness is retained as water. This may be specific or general in location. It causes us to swell, to become waterlogged.

Phlegm

This describes a more sticky manifestation of Dampness. It often lodges in particular organs and combines easily with Heat or Cold. Phlegm, or Mucus, congeals and obstructs our functioning.

Resolving Dampness Through Food

All Dampness is treated by strengthening the Spleen and may also need tonification of the Kidney, the Lung and the Yang. Phlegm demands the reduction of Phlegm-forming foods and the use of Phlegm-resolving foods. Water is helped by Water-removing (diuretic) foods.

Dampness is often the result of overeating or overnutrition. It may also result from jamming the digestive system with poorly combined foods. All the advice on supporting the Spleen earlier in this book is important in avoiding the overaccumulation of Dampness.

In particular we need to avoid too much raw, cold, sweet or rich food and the overconsumption of fluid. Some foods are particularly dampening. They are as follows:

Dairy products (sheep and goat products are less dampening), Pork and rich meat, Saturated fats, Roasted Peanuts, Concentrated juices especially Orange and Tomato, Wheatflour, Bread, Yeast, Beer, Bananas, Sugar and sweeteners.

Some foods, on the other hand, have properties which help to resolve Dampness. They are as follows:

Foods which resolve Dampness

Aduki bean	*Caraway*	*Green Tea*	*Marjoram*	*Radish*
Alfalfa	*Cardamom*	*Horseradish*	*Mushroom(button)*	*Rye*
Anchovy	*Celery*	*Jasmine tea*	*Mustard leaf*	*Scallion*
Asparagus	*Clove*	*Job's Tears*	*Onion*	*Turnip*
Barley	*Coriander*	*Kidney bean*	*Oregano*	*Umeboshi*
Basil	*Corn*	*Kohlrabi*	*Parsley*	*Plum*
Buckwheat	*Daikon*	*Lemon*	*Pumpkin*	
Buckwheat tea	*Garlic*	*Mackerel*	*Quail*	

Foods which resolve Water

Aduki bean	*Broad bean*	*Frog*	*Mackerel*	*Sardine*
Alfalfa	*Celery*	*Grape*	*Mungbean*	*Seaweed*
Anchovy	*Clam*	*Job's Tears*	*Pea*	*Squash*
Asparagus	*Fenugreek*	*Kelp*	*Plantain*	*Tea*
Barley	*Corn-on-the-cob*	*Kidney bean*	*Plum*	*Watercress*
Basil	*Cornsilk*	*Lettuce*	*Raspberry leaf*	*Water Chestnut*
Black Soybean	*Duck*	*Loach*	*Rice*	

Foods which resolve Phlegm

Almond	*Grapefruit*	*Mustard leaf*	*Peppermint*	*Tangerine peel*
Apple peel	*Grapefruit peel*	*Mustard seed*	*Persimmon*	*Tea*
Black Pepper	*Laver*	*Olive*	*Plantain*	*Thyme*
Celery	*Lemon peel*	*Onion*	*Radish*	*Walnut*
Clam	*Licorice*	*Orange peel*	*Seaweed*	*Watercress*
Daikon	*Marjoram*	*Pear*	*Shiitake*	
Garlic	*Mushroom(button)*	*Pepper*	*Shrimp*	

COLD

A condition of Cold frequently arises from a deficiency of Yang (see page 24) but it is possible for Cold to take hold in the body without this predisposition. Cold can literally penetrate the body from the environment and lodge there, causing contraction and obstruction. This may occur in the muscles and joints and even in organs such as the Stomach, Intestines, Uterus and Bladder when exposed to cold temperatures. It can also penetrate to the interior of the body through the overconsumption of cold foods or liquids.

Another way Cold can penetrate is as a pathogen such as a virus. If the Cold influence is not driven off, it may lodge deeper in the body becoming chronic. Heat may also transform into Cold over time and vice-versa.

At the emotional level Cold arises from fear which causes us to contract, inhibiting our ability to flow and act freely. Cold may also be the result of long-held unexpressed emotions such as love, grief and anger, and of old emotional injury and trauma.

Cold causes contraction and obstructs the flow of blood and energy, sometimes painfully. To ward off Cold we need to be sufficiently physically active, keep warmly clothed, apply warmth to any affected areas and, if appropriate, work on our fears and old emotional wounds.

Driving Out Cold Through Food

At the dietary level we can favour more warming methods of food preparation and eat foods with warming properties. For chronic conditions we use warm and sweet foods. In acute stages of Cold invasion we can use warm and pungent foods to drive the Cold to the body surface, even to the extent of causing sweating. Foods which are especially effective in driving off Cold are listed below.

Amasake	*Chestnut*	*Goat Milk*	*Mustard seed*	*Spearmint*
Anchovy	*Chicken*	*Ginger*	*Mutton*	*Squash*
Basil	*Chive seed*	*Kohlrabi*	*Nutmeg*	*Sweet Rice*
Bay	*Cinnamon*	*Lamb*	*Onion*	*Trout*
Black Pepper	*Clove*	*Lamb Kidney*	*Peach*	*Turnip*
Brown Sugar	*Coriander seed*	*Leek*	*Pine kernel*	*Vinegar*
Butter	*Date*	*Lychee*	*Rosemary*	*Walnut*
Caper	*Dill seed*	*Longan*	*Scallion*	*Wine*
Cardamom	*Fennel seed*	*Malt Sugar*	*Shrimp*	
Cayenne	*Garlic*	*Mussel*	*Sorghum*	
Cherry	*Goat*	*Mustard leaf*	*Soya oil*	

HEAT

There are several ways that we can become hot. We may suddenly contract an acute feverish illness indicating that a "hot" pathogen has penetrated our defences. If we do not expel this invasion the Heat may lodge deeper in our body causing inflammation and irritation. The initial stage of invasion is called Wind-Heat in Chinese medicine.

Heat may also arise from prolonged overconsumption of heating foods or substances. It may arise from over-activity or prolonged strain on all or part of our system. It may also arise from prolonged exposure to a hot environment. At the emotional level it arises from feelings which cannot be resolved or expressed. Heat combines easily with Dampness and is often a sequel to periods of Stagnation.

The above descriptions all refer to the condition of "Full Heat". It is vitally important to distinguish between this condition and that of "Empty Heat". Empty Heat arises when over a period of time our Yin becomes deficient. The cooling, lubricating function and the quality of our fuel becomes depleted. In this case we become hot because we cannot keep cool.

Empty Heat needs tonification of Yin (see page 23). Full Heat needs cooling or expelling.

Removing Heat Through Food

In chronic conditions Heat is simply treated by the avoidance of hot foods and the use of more cooling foods and methods of food preparation. Where there is a pathogenic invasion the pungent flavour is used to drive the hot invader to the surface of the body. Some Heat-reducing foods are listed below.

Alfalfa	*Cabbage*	*Grapefruit*	*Olive*	*Spirulina*
Apple	*Celery*	*Kelp*	*Pear*	*Tofu*
Asparagus	*Chard*	*Lemon*	*Peppermint*	*Tomato*
Aubergine	*Chinese Cabbage*	*Lettuce*	*Persimmon*	*Watermelon*
Bamboo Shoot	*Clam*	*Millet*	*Potato*	*Wheat*
Banana	*Cucumber*	*Mint*	*Radish*	
Barley	*Egg white*	*Mung bean*	*Salt*	
Broccoli	*Elderflower*	*Mung beansprout*	*Seaweed*	

WIND

When the body is invaded by a pathogen such as the common cold, influenza or laryngitis this is often referred to as an invasion of Wind. Wind easily combines with the previous conditions of Heat, Cold and Dampness. Its behaviour, as in nature, is characterised by its sudden onset and erratic symptoms such as wandering pains or alternating chills and fever. The Lung is frequently the first Organ to be attacked.

Wind invasion is treated through use of the pungent flavour which assists the body to expel pathogens by directing Qi outwards. This is combined with foods which counteract the influences of Heat, Cold and Dampness.

Driving Out Wind Through Food

All invasions of Wind are best treated by simplifying the diet and cutting out all congesting foods such as dairy, rich meat, bread, saturated fat and sugar. These foods may draw the illness more deeply into the body and create Phlegm. Instead it is better to favour light soups and adequate rest. Helpful foods are listed below.

Wind Heat

Borage	*Chinese Cabbage*	*Eucalyptus*	*Mint*	*Spearmint*
Burdock root	*Chrysanthemum*	*Lemon Balm*	*Oregano*	*Turnip*
Catnip	*Echinacea*	*Limeflower*	*Peppermint*	*Yarrow*
Chamomile	*Elderflower*	*Marjoram*	*Sage*	

Wind Cold

Basil	*Chilli*	*Ginger (fresh)*	*Peppermint*
Black Pepper	*Cinnamon*	*Leek*	*Rosemary*
Caraway	*Coriander leaf*	*Mustard leaf*	*Sage*
Cayenne	*Garlic*	*Onion*	*Scallion*

Wind Damp

Basil	*Job's Tears*	*Onion family*	*Spearmint*	*Turnip*
Cayenne	*Juniper*	*Peppermint*	*Tangerine peel*	
Cherry	*Kohlrabi*	*Radish*	*Thyme*	
Eel	*Mustard leaf*	*Rosemary*	*Turmeric*	

QI STAGNATION

When the Qi moves freely our lives flow easily. We adapt to change, process difficulties and heal from illness. Sometimes the Qi can become blocked and aspects of our lives, either physical or emotional, become blocked too.

At the physical level this can mean that an Organ and its associated functions jam up, and a queue of problems starts to form behind the blockage. As with traffic queues this can lead to frustration, anger or even reckless behaviour in search of a way out. Problems start to accumulate in the stuck place in the body/psyche then start to erupt elsewhere as the Qi looks for escape routes. Stagnant Qi in the Liver, for example, might escape up the Gall Bladder meridian causing crashing headaches, or move sideways into the digestive system and cause chaos there.

The cause of Qi Stagnation is most often emotional. Feelings and creative impulses which we are unable to process create blockage. At a physical level Qi Stagnation is aggravated by lack of movement. Movement, at any level of our being, is the key to working with stagnation.

Promoting Qi Circulation Through Food

We can assist the circulation of Qi to some extent through how and what we eat. To avoid stagnation it is important not to overeat and not to consume too much heavy food at any one time. We also need to avoid sugar and stimulants which may appear to give temporary relief but eventually worsen the root of the problem.

Chewing food well will help its passage through the digestive system. To encourage movement we can also include some of the pungent foods and herbs that stimulate the dispersal of Qi. In choosing pungent foods we need to take into account whether Heat, Cold or Deficiency are bound up with the stagnation. See the relevant sections for guidelines.

Foods which especially help the circulation of Qi are listed below.

Basil	*Clove*	*Kohlrabi*	*Plum*	*Turnip*
Caraway	*Coriander*	*Marjoram*	*Radish*	*Vinegar*
Cardamom	*Dill seed*	*Mustard leaf*	*Squash*	*Watercress*
Carrot	*Fennel*	*Orange peel*	*Star Anise*	
Cayenne	*Garlic*	*Peach*	*Tangerine peel*	
Chive	*Grapefruit*	*Peppermint*	*Turmeric*	

BLOOD STAGNATION

Stagnant Blood describes a condition where the circulation of Blood is blocked or restricted. Stagnant Blood is treated in much the same way as Stagnant Qi. It is often the result of Stagnant Qi manifesting in more tangible, physical form.

Unless there is injury, tumour or severe exhaustion, both physical and emotional movement are part of the long-term remedy.

Promoting Blood Circulation Through Food

Advice for Blood Stagnation is largely the same as for Qi Stagnation. Levels of toxicity and fat stored in the Blood will also contribute to stagnation, so it is generally best to support attempts to move Blood Stagnation with foods that maintain and improve Blood quality.

Note also that foods which move Blood are often warm in nature so it is important to be cautious if signs of Heat are also present. Foods which especially help move the Blood are listed below.

Amasake	*Chicken Egg*	*Kohlrabi*	*Radish*	*Sweet Rice*
Aubergine	*Chilli Pepper*	*Leek*	*Saffron*	*Rose*
Brown Sugar	*Chive*	*Mustard leaf*	*Scallion*	*Turmeric*
Butter	*Crab*	*Onion*	*Shark*	*Turnip*
Chestnut	*Hawthorn Berry*	*Peach*	*Sturgeon*	*Vinegar*

SHEN

Shen means spirit or consciousness. It is the light of the body which is reflected in the eyes, the spiritual essence of a person. Although it has no substance, Shen is rooted in the life of the physical body but can also both transcend and influence the life of the body. For example, our Shen can be affected by what we eat, by foods and substances which alter our energy, mood and behaviour. Our Shen can also transform physical difficulty by bringing the light of consciousness to any aspect of the body.

Our Shen is said to reside in the Heart and the Blood. This is a way of saying that consciousness is not located in the brain but circulates through the whole body and that the most important Organ, the Heart, is where we integrate our experience of life, transforming our experience into the light of consciousness. The cultivation of Shen is the goal of spiritual practice.

When our Shen is healthy we are in a state of psycholgical integrity in which the mind is clear-seeing, we have a good grip on reality and consciousness is properly anchored in the physical body. Our Shen can be disturbed by stress, by traumatic experiences or by psychoactive substances and made restless by under-nutrition or over-stimulation, or depressed by lack of contact with life.

It is easier to cultivate Shen when the foundations of our physical and energetic body are strong. Therefore, like everything else, Shen is affected by nutrition. As the Romans put it, "mens sana in corpore sano" (a healthy mind in a healthy body). Some foods are known for their influence on the Shen in the sense of either calming or raising the Spirit. Strong substances may be used in herbalism such as magnetite, cinnabar or pearl but they need careful and skilled management to avoid toxic effects. In western medicine some vitamins and minerals such as Vitamin C, Folic acid, Calcium, Magnesium and Selenium can be said to calm the Spirit. A few of the milder acting foods and herbs are listed below.

Foods which calm the Spirit and relieve anxiety

Bitter Orange flower	*Frankincense*	*Lavender*	*Motherwort*	*Valerian*
Celery	*Hops*	*Lettuce*	*Mulberry*	*Warm milk*
Chamomile	*Jamaican Dogwood*	*Mistletoe*	*Sandalwood*	*Wheat*

Foods which raise the Spirit and lift depression

Arnica flower	*Gingko*	*Melissa*	*Rosemary*	*Scullcap*
Basil	*Ginseng*	*Oat*	*Sage*	*Tea*
Bilberry	*Jasmine*	*Rose*	*St. John's Wort*	

PART THREE

*The Energetics of Food
Reference Chart*

ABBREVIATIONS

Route

L	Lung
LI	Large Intestine
St	Stomach
S	Spleen
H	Heart
SI	Small Intestine
B	Bladder
K	Kidney
Liv	Liver
GB	Gall Bladder
Pe	Pericardium
TH	Triple Heater
U	Uterus

Action

QC	Promotes Qi Circulation
BC	Promotes Blood Circulation
C	Counteracts Cold
H	Counteracts Heat
D	Counteracts Damp
DC	Counteracts Damp Cold
DH	Counteracts Damp Heat
W	Drains Water
P	Resolves Phlegm
T	Removes Toxins
WC	Reduces Wind Cold
WH	Reduces Wind Heat
WD	Reduces Wind Damp
WDC	Reduces Wind Damp Cold

Grains

Grains provide basic nourishment for the Blood and Qi. They provide a stable release of energy and are generally easy to digest, especially in cereal form i.e. as porridge. Bitterness can be found in the outer layers giving many whole grains an ability to mildly drain Dampness. Cooler grains such as barley are effective at reducing Heat, while warmer grains such as oats will help remove Coldness. When grains are milled into flour they can become slightly dampening.

FOOD	TEMP	FLAVOUR	ROUTE	TONIFIES	REGULATES
Amaranth	Cool	Sweet, Bitter	L Li Liv B	Qi	D W
Barley	Cool	Sweet, Salty	S St GB B Int	Blood, Yin, Qi	W D H T
Buckwheat	Cool	Sweet	LI S St		D H QC
Corn (maize)	Neutral	Sweet	K LI St	Qi	W
Job's Tears (coix)	Cool	Sweet	L LI K S St GB	Blood, Qi	D H W *WD*
Kamut	Cool	Sweet	H K S	Yin	H
Millet	Cool	Sweet, Salty	K S St	Yin	H T
Oats	Warm	Sweet	K S St H L LI	Qi, Blood	QC
Quinoa	Warm	Sweet, Sour	K Pe	Yang, Qi	
Rice	Neutral	Sweet	S St	Qi, Blood	
Rice, sweet	Warm	Sweet	S St L	Blood, Qi	BC C
Rice, wild	Cool	Sweet, Sour	K B		
Rye	Neutral	Sweet, Bitter	GB Liv S H	Qi	D W QC
Seitan (gluten)	Cool	Sweet	St S Liv	Qi	H
Sorghum	Warm	Sweet	LI L S St		C D DH
Spelt	Warm	Sweet	S	Yin	
Wheat	Cool	Sweet	H K S	Yin	H
Wheat bran	Cool	Sweet	LI St		H D
Wheat germ	Cold	Sweet, Pungent	H SI	Blood, Qi	BC H

Vegetables

FOOD	TEMP	FLAVOUR	ROUTE	TONIFIES	REGULATES
Alfalfa sprout	Cool	Bitter, Salty	K LI S St	Yin, Blood	D W H DH T
Artichoke, globe	Neutral	Bitter, Salty, Sweet	GB Liv	Yin, Blood	QC W D DH
Asparagus	Cool	Bitter, Sweet, Pungent	K L S	Yin	D H DH W T
Aubergine	Cool	Sweet	LI Liv S St U		BC H
Bamboo shoot	Cool	Sweet, Bitter	LI L St		D H W P
Beetroot	Neutral	Sweet	H Liv Int	Blood	QC C
Bok choy	Cool	Sweet, Sour	St LI		H W T
Broccoli	Cool	Bitter, Pungent, Sweet	Liv St S B		QC H W
Brussels sprout	Warm	Sweet, Pungent	St LI		C
Burdock Root	Cool	Pungent, Bitter	L Int.B K St		*WH* H D T
Cabbage	Neutral	Pungent, Sweet	LI St L		H QC
Caper	Warm	Bitter, Pungent			BC C D W
Carrot	Neutral	Sweet	Liv L S	Qi	QC H T DH
Cauliflower	Neutral	Sweet, Bitter	LI S St SI		
Celery	Cool	Bitter, Sweet	Liv St K B		D H W DH
Chard, Swiss	Cool	Sweet	LI L S St	Blood	H T
Chicory	Cool	Bitter	GB Liv		W
Chinese cabbage	Cool	Sweet	St L LI		D H W DH
Courgette	Cool	Sweet	S St L		H
Coriander leaf	Warm	Pungent	L S St		BC QC *WC*
Cucumber	Cold	Sweet	LI S St B		H T
Daikon	Cool	Pungent, Sweet	L		D P
Dandelion leaf	Cold	Bitter, Salty, Sweet	GB Liv S	Blood	H W DH
Endive	Cool	Bitter, Sweet	H LI		H DH
Fennel bulb	Warm	Pungent	Liv K S St		C
Jerusalem artichoke	Neutral	Sweet	L S LI		
Kale	Warm	Bitter, Sweet	L St	Blood	
Kohlrabi	Neutral	Bitter, Pungent, Sweet	S St		QC BC D T W
Leek	Warm	Pungent, Sweet, Sour	Liv S St L		BC QC C

Vegetables have a wide range of actions and are essential for our health: root vegetables tend to be sweet, nourishing to the Spleen and mildly active against Dampness; leafy greens provide essential nutrients for the Blood; the onion family helps to counter Stagnation and Coldness, and so on. Eating a wide range of vegetables will support our energy, keep the intestines healthy and counter obesity and degenerative diseases.

FOOD	TEMP	FLAVOUR	ROUTE	TONIFIES	REGULATES
Lettuce	Cool	Bitter, Sweet	LI St		D H W QC
Lotus root	Cold	Sweet	H S St		H QC
Marrow	Cool	Sweet	S St		
Mungbean sprout	Cold	Sweet	LI	Yin	H T
Mushroom, button	Cool	Sweet	LI L SI St		P QC H T
Mustard leaf	Warm	Pungent	L St S		BC QC C P W
Olive	Neutral	Sour, Sweet	L St		H DH T
Onion	Warm	Pungent	L St Liv LI		BC C D P QC
Parsnip	Warm	Pungent, Sweet	Liv L S St		D
Pepper, bell	Warm	Pungent, Sweet	St K		BC C
Plantain	Cold	Sweet	LI SI Liv S		H P W
Potato	Neutral	Sweet	K S St	Qi, Yin	H
Pumpkin	Warm	Sweet	L LI S St	Qi	BC C D P
Radish	Cool	Pungent, Sweet	L St		D P QC H T
Scallion	Warm	Bitter, Pungent	H LI L St	Yang	BC C D WC T
Seaweed	Cold	Salty	K St	Yin	H P D W T
Spinach	Cool	Sweet	LI St Liv	Blood, Yin	H
Squash, summer	Cool	Sweet	L LI S St	Yin	W H T
Squash, winter	Warm	Sweet	L LI S St	Qi	BC C D P
String bean	Neutral	Sweet	K S	Yin	
Sweet potato	Neutral	Sweet	K S St LI	Qi, Blood, Yin	T
Taro	Neutral	Sweet, Pungent	S St		
Tomato	Cold	Sour, Sweet	Liv St	Yin	H T
Turnip	Neutral	Bitter, Pungent, Sweet	St S L		BC QC P D H
Water chestnut	Cold	Sweet	LI B S L St Liv		H P W
Watercress	Cool	Bitter, Pungent	LI L S St B K	Blood, Qi	P QC W H D
Yam	Neutral	Sweet	K L S	Yin, Qi	

Fungus

Fungi can provide a valuable source of less common minerals such as germanium. From the viewpoint of Chinese medicine, fungi often have some action against Dampness, support the immune system and counter the progression of degenerative diseases. They combine well with meat, helping to deal with some of its toxins.

FOOD	TEMP	FLAVOUR	ROUTE	TONIFIES	REGULATES
Ceps (boletus)	Neutral	Salty	K Liv		H
Field Mushroom (agaricus)	Cold	Sweet	S St L		P
Oyster Mushroom	Warm	Sweet	S St Liv		D
Puffball, giant	Neutral	Pungent	L		H
Reishi	Warm	Sweet	H	Qi, Blood	
Shiitake	Neutral	Sweet	St S Liv	Qi, Blood	P
Wood Ear (Black Fungus)	Neutral	Sweet	L St Liv	Yin	BC H

Seaweeds

Seaweeds are an excellent source of minerals. They nourish the Yin and Blood, remove toxins and clear both Dampness and Heat. They also help improve the digestibility of legumes through their softening action. They are a good way of including the salty flavour in the diet.

FOOD	TEMP	FLAVOUR	ROUTE	TONIFIES	REGULATES
Agar	Cold	Sweet, Salty	L Liv LI		H P
Arame	Cool	Salty			
Dulse	Cool	Salty			
Hijiki	Cool	Salty			W PH T
Irish Moss	Cool	Salty	L		P H
Kelp/Kombu	Cold	Salty	K Liv St L	Yin, Blood	W P H T
Laver	Cold	Sweet, Salty	Liv L St K		H P W
Nori	Cool	Sweet, Salty		Yin	W H P
Wakame	Cool	Salty		Yin	W PH

Fruits

FOOD	TEMP	FLAVOUR	ROUTE	TONIFIES	REGULATES
Apple	Cool	Sour, Sweet	H L St S Ll	Yin, Qi	H T
Apricot	Neutral	Sour, Sweet	Ll L St	Yin, Blood	
Avocado	Cool	Sweet	Ll L Liv S	Yin, Blood	
Banana	Cold	Sweet	Ll L St S	Yin	H T
Blackberry	Warm	Sour, Sweet	Liv K		
Blackcurrant	Cool	Sour, Sweet	Liv K		
Blue/bilberry	Cool	Sour, Sweet	L S St		D H T
Carambola	Neutral	Sour, Sweet	St S Ll L B	Yin	
Cherry	Warm	Sweet	H S St Liv L K	Qi, Blood	BC C *WDC*
Crabapple	Neutral	Sour, Sweet	H Liv L		
Cranberry	Cold	Sour, Sweet	B K Ll		D H DH
Date	Warm	Sweet	Liv L S	Qi, Blood	
Fig	Neutral	Sweet	Ll L S St	Qi, Blood	H T
Gooseberry	Cold	Sour, Sweet	Liv		
Grape	Neutral	Sour, Sweet	K Liv L S St	Qi, Blood	W
Grapefruit	Cold	Sour, Sweet	St S L		H P QC
Grapefruit peel	Warm	Bitter, Sweet	S K B		D P QC
Guava	Warm	Sour, Sweet	L Ll S St		
Kiwi	Cool	Sour, Sweet	St S B		H
Kumquat	Warm	Pungent, Sour, Sweet	St S Liv		P QC D
Lemon/Lime	Cold	Sour	GB Liv K L S		BC QC H T P
Lemon peel	Warm	Pungent, Bitter	S L		D P QC
Longan	Warm	Sweet	H S	Qi, Blood	BC QC C
Loquat	Cool	Sour, Sweet	L S St		H
Lychee	Warm	Sour, Sweet	Liv S St	Blood	BC QC C
Mandarin	Cool	Sour, Sweet	L S		P H W
Mango	Cool	Sour, Sweet	St S L	Yin	H QC W
Melon	Cold	Sweet	L		H
Mulberry	Cold	Sweet	K Liv L S	Yin, Blood, Qi	W H T

Fruit provides fluids and their moist, lubricating action makes them supportive of the Yin and beneficial for the colon. The cooling nature of most fruits also makes them effective against internal Heat and their generally alkalizing nature helps balance acidic blood. Fruit also supplies useful nutrients for the formation of Blood and Qi. People with Hot, Dry and Yin Deficient conditions especially benefit from eating more fruit.

FOOD	TEMP	FLAVOUR	ROUTE	TONIFIES	REGULATES
Orange	Cool	Sour, Sweet	Liv L St	Yin	QC
Orange peel	Warm	Sour, Bitter	L S St		QC D P
Papaya (Pawpaw)	Neutral	Sweet	L St S	Qi	D BC P
Peach	Warm	Sour, Sweet	LI SI St	Yin	BC QC C
Pear	Cool	Sour, Sweet	L St S	Yin	H P
Persimmon	Cold	Sweet, Sour	H LI L S St	Yin	H P
Pineapple	Neutral	Sour, Sweet	St S B	Yin	H W *WD*
Plum	Neutral	Sour, Sweet	Liv St S LI B	Yin	H QC W
Pomegranate	Neutral	Sour, Sweet	B St S LI L	Yin	H
Pomelo	Cool	Sour, Sweet	S St L		P T W D
Quince	Warm	Sour	Liv S St		D
Raspberry	Warm	Sour, Sweet	Liv K	Yin	
Rhubarb	Cold	Bitter	LI		BC H T
Strawberry	Cool	Sour, Sweet	K Liv L S St	Yin	
Tamarind	Cool	Sour, Sweet	St LI		H
Tangerine	Cool	Sour, Sweet	L St S		QC H
Tangerine peel	Warm	Pungent, Bitter	S L		D P QC
Umeboshi plum	Warm	Sour	LI L S Liv	Qi	
Watermelon	Cold	Sweet	B H St		H W

Beans

Beans provide deep nourishment for the Blood, Yin and Qi, and support for the Kidney. They are nourishing without being dampening and many beans, especially the smaller beans such as aduki, are effective at draining Dampness and Water. They combine particularly well with grains to make excellent nourishment for the Blood and their digestibility improves by combination with seaweeds or aromatic herbs and spices.

FOOD	TEMP	FLAVOUR	ROUTE	TONIFIES	REGULATES
Aduki bean	Neutral	Sour, Sweet	H K Sl S	Blood	D W H BC T
Black bean	Warm	Sweet	K	Yin, Blood	W
Blackeye bean	Neutral	Sweet	S St B		D W
Broad bean (fava)	Neutral	Sweet	S St K		D
Chickpea (garbanzo)	Neutral	Sweet	H St S	Qi	D
Kidney bean	Neutral	Sweet	K S LI Sl	Yin, Blood	D H W
Lentil	Neutral	Sweet	H K S St	Qi	D W
Lima bean	Cool	Sweet	Liv L	Yin	
Mung bean	Cool	Sweet	H St	Yin	H DH W T
Pea	Neutral	Sweet	S St H LI	Yin	W
Soybean, black	Neutral	Sweet	K S Liv LI	Yin, Blood	W BC T
Soybean, yellow	Cool	Sweet	LI S St	Qi, Blood	H T
Tempeh	Warm	Sweet		Qi, Blood	
Tofu	Cold	Sweet	LI S St	Yin, Qi	H T

Nuts & Seeds

Nuts and seeds are particularly nourishing to the Yin. They provide nourishing and lubricating oils which benefit the intestines and nourish the Liver. Because of their oily nature, over-consumption can cause the accumulation of Dampness.

FOOD	TEMP	FLAVOUR	ROUTE	TONIFIES	REGULATES
Almond	Neutral	Sweet	L Ll S	Qi, Jing	P QC
Cashew	Neutral	Sweet	L		
Chestnut	Warm	Sweet	K S St	Yang, Qi	BC
Coconut	Warm	Sweet	H S St Ll	Qi, Blood	
Coconut milk	Neutral	Sweet	H	Yin	C
Flax (linseed)	Neutral	Sweet	Ll S Liv	Yin	
Gingko	Neutral	Bitter, Sweet	L S K		
Hazel	Neutral	Sweet	St S	Qi, Blood	
Hemp seed	Neutral	Sweet	S St Ll	Yin	
Peanut	Neutral	Sweet	L S	Blood, Qi	W P
Pine kernel	Warm	Sweet	Ll L liv	Yin, Qi	BC C
Pistachio	Neutral	Bitter, Sour, Sweet	K Liv Int	Yang, Qi	
Poppy seed	Neutral	Sweet	St K		
Pumpkin seed	Warm	Bitter, Sweet	Ll S St		W
Sesame, black	Neutral	Sweet	K Liv Int	Yin, Blood, Jing	
Sesame, white	Neutral	Sweet	K Liv Int	Yin, Blood, Jing	
Sunflower seed	Neutral	Sweet	S Int	Qi	
Walnut	Warm	Sweet	K L Int	Yang, Qi, Jing	C P

Fish

Fish are an excellent source of nourishment. Fish strengthens weakness in the body and supports the formation of vibrant Qi and Blood. Those with Yin deficient conditions will especially benefit from eating more fish.

FOOD	TEMP	FLAVOUR	ROUTE	TONIFIES	REGULATES
Abalone	Neutral	Salty, Sweet	Liv K	Yin, Jing	H
Anchovy	Warm	Sweet, Salty	S St	Yang, Qi	C D W
Carp	Neutral	Sweet	S St Liv K	Blood, Qi	W
Clam (freshwater)	Cold	Salty, Sweet	K Liv	Yin	H
Clam (saltwater)	Cold	Salty	St	Yin	H P
Crab	Cold	Salty	Liv St	Yin	BC H D DH
Cuttlefish	Neutral	Salty, Sweet	H K Liv	Yin, Blood	
Eel	Warm	Sweet	K Liv S L	Qi, Yin, Blood	D WDC Wind
Frog	Cool	Sweet	B LI SI St	Qi	H T W
Herring	Neutral	Sweet	L S	Qi	T
Loach	Neutral	Sweet	S K	Qi, Yang	D
Lobster & Crayfish	Warm	Salty, Sweet	K Liv	Yang	P
Mackerel	Neutral	Sweet	Liv St	Qi	D W
Mullet	Cold	Sweet	St S	Qi, Yin	W
Mussel	Warm	Salty	K Liv	Yang, Blood, Jing	BC C
Octopus	Cold	Salty, Sweet		Yin, Qi, Blood	H
Oyster	Neutral	Salty, Sweet	K Liv	Yin, Qi, Blood, Jing	
Perch	Neutral	Sweet	S St Liv K		
Salmon	Warm	Sweet	S St	Qi, Blood	
Sardine	Neutral	Salty, Sweet	S St	Qi, Yin	W
Scallop	Neutral	Sweet, Salty	K	Yin	
Shark	Neutral	Salty, Sweet	S St K Liv H L	Qi, Blood	BC
Shrimp & Prawn	Warm	Sweet	K Liv S St	Yang, Qi	BC C P
Squid	Neutral	Salty, Sweet	Liv K	Blood	
Sturgeon	Neutral	Sweet	L P S	Qi	BC
Trout	Hot	Sour	St Liv GB	Qi, Yang	C
Tuna	Neutral	Sweet	St S	Qi, Blood	D
Whitebait	Neutral	Sweet	St S	Yin	
Whitefish	Neutral	Sweet	Liv L S St		

Meat

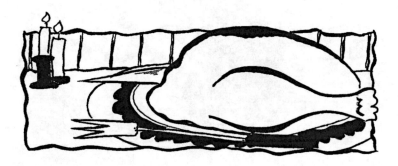

Meat is deeply nourishing to the Blood and will increase the warmth and energy in the body. It tends to be warming and somewhat moistening therefore over-consumption tends to result in the accumulation of Heat and Dampness. Those who are Blood Deficient or who lack warmth will benefit most from eating meat.

FOOD	TEMP	FLAVOUR	ROUTE	TONIFIES	REGULATES
Beef	Warm	Sweet	LI S St Liv	Yin, Qi, Blood	
Beef, kidney	Warm	Sweet	K	Yang, Jing	
Beef, liver	Neutral	Sweet	Liv	Blood	
Beef, tripe	Neutral	Sweet	St S	Qi	
Chicken	Warm	Sweet	S St K	Qi, Blood, Jing	BC C
Chicken, liver	Warm	Sweet	K Liv	Qi, Yin	BC
Duck	Neutral	Sweet, Salty	K L St S	Yin, Qi, Blood	W D
Goat	Warm	Sweet	K S	Qi, Yang, Blood	C
Goose	Neutral	Sweet	L S	Yin, Qi	
Ham	Warm	Salty	S	Qi	
Lamb	Hot	Sweet	K S	Yang, Qi, Blood	C
Lamb, kidney	Warm	Sweet	K	Yang, Qi, Jing	BC C QC
Lamb, liver	Cool	Sweet, Bitter	Liv	Blood	
Mutton	Warm	Sweet	K S	Qi, Yang, Blood	C
Pheasant	Warm	Sour, Sweet	H St	Qi	
Pigeon	Neutral	Sweet, Salty	Liv K	Yin, Qi, Blood	
Pork	Neutral	Sweet, Salty	K S St Liv	Yin, Blood, Qi	
Pork, heart	Neutral	Sweet, Salty	H	Qi	
Pork, kidney	Neutral	Salty	K	Yin, Jing	
Pork, liver	Warm	Sweet, Bitter	Liv	Blood	
Pork, tripe	Warm	Sweet	S St		
Pork, trotter	Neutral	Sweet	St	Qi, Blood	
Quail	Neutral	Sweet	LI S St Liv	Qi, Blood	D W H
Rabbit	Cool	Sweet	LI Liv S St	Yin, Qi	
Turkey	Warm	Sweet	S St	Qi	
Venison	Warm	Sweet	Liv K	Yang, Qi	

Dairy

Dairy foods provide a rich source of nourishment and, for this reason, should be treated with respect. Their over-consumption easily leads to the accumulation of Phlegm and Dampness. However, they are very strengthening for the Yin, Blood and Qi and will effectively nourish Deficiency in the body.

FOOD	TEMP	FLAVOUR	ROUTE	TONIFIES	REGULATES
Butter	Warm	Sweet	S St	Yin	BC C
Cheese	Neutral	Sour, Sweet	L Liv S	Yin, Qi, Blood	
Egg, chicken	Neutral	Sweet	H K L St S Liv	Yin, Blood, Jing	BC
Egg, duck	Cool	Sweet	H L St	Yin, Jing	
Egg, pigeon	Neutral	Sweet, Salty	K H	Yin, Jing	
Egg, quail	Neutral	Sweet	Liv K S	Qi, Blood, Jing	
Egg white	Neutral	Sweet	L		H
Egg yolk	Neutral	Sweet	H K Liv	Yin, Blood	
Ghee	Warm	Sweet	S St	Yin, Jing	
Milk, cow	Neutral	Sweet	H L St	Yin, Qi, Blood	
Milk, cow (raw)	Warm	Sweet	H L St	Yin, Qi, Blood, Jing	
Milk, goat/sheep	Warm	Sweet	St L K	Yin, Qi, Blood, Jing	
Yoghourt	Cold	Sour, Sweet	L Liv St LI	Yin, Qi, Blood	

Culinary Herbs & Spices

Herbs and spices have a wide variety of actions. Their properties are more concentrated than those of most foods. They can be used to improve the digestibility of foods, moderate their energetics or to direct the healing properties of a recipe. Aromatic herbs benefit digestion by stimulating the Spleen. Pungent flavoured herbs help move the Blood and Qi. Herbs can also help resolve Dampness and Phlegm, drive out Cold and combat Wind invasions. The use of herbs and spices can increase the nutritional value of a meal as well as making it taste good.

FOOD	TEMP	FLAVOUR	ROUTE	TONIFIES	REGULATES
Asafoetida	Warm	Pungent, Bitter	Liv S St		C P
Aniseed	Warm	Pungent, Sweet	H L S St Liv K	Yang, Qi	D P QC
Basil	Warm	Bitter, Pungent, Sweet	K L S St Ll	Yang	D P C QC *WC*
Bay	Warm	Pungent			BC C
Caraway	Warm	Pungent, Sweet	B K St		P QC *WC* C
Cardamom	Warm	Pungent, Bitter, Sweet	St S L Ll		D P QC C
Carob	Warm	Sour, Sweet			
Cayenne	Hot	Pungent	L S St H	Yang	BC QC *WDC*
Chilli	Hot	Pungent	L S St H	Yang	BC QC *WDC*
Chive leaf	Warm	Pungent	K Liv St		BC QC
Chive seed	Warm	Pungent, Salty	K Liv	Yang	C
Cinnamon bark	Hot	Pungent, Sweet	K L S H U	Yang, Qi	C D QC BC
Clove	Warm	Pungent	K S St	Yang	C QC
Coriander seed	Neutral	Pungent, Sour	St		C QC
Cumin	Warm	Pungent	Liv S		
Dill seed	Warm	Pungent	K S St	Yang	C QC
Fennel seed	Warm	Pungent, Sweet	B K S St Liv	Yang, Qi	C P QC
Fenugreek seed	Warm	Bitter, Pungent, Sweet	K Liv S L	Yang	QC W D C
Galangal	Hot	Pungent	S St		C
Garlic	Hot	Pungent, Salty, Sweet	H Liv L S St	Yang	D P QC *WC* T
Ginger (dry)	Hot	Pungent, Sweet	L S St Int H U	Yang	BC QC C P
Ginger (fresh)	Hot	Pungent, Sweet	L S St Int H U		C P QC *WC*

Culinary Herbs & Spices *(continued)*

FOOD	TEMP	FLAVOUR	ROUTE	TONIFIES	REGULATES
Hawthorn	Warm	Sour, Sweet	H Liv Pe S St	Qi	BC QC
Horseradish	Hot	Pungent	B K L St S	Yang	D P C QC *WDC*
Juniper	Warm	Pungent, Sweet, Sour	S K B L LI Liv		DH P QC *WDC*
Licorice	Neutral	Sweet	all	Qi	H P T QC
Marjoram	Cool	Bitter, Pungent, Sweet	L S St	Yin	QC *WH*
Marigold	Cool	Bitter	St Int		H
Mint	Cool	Pungent	L Liv		*WH* QC
Mustard	Hot	Pungent	L		P QC
Nettle	Cool	Salty, Sweet	B K Liv S	Yin, Blood, Jing	D T W
Nutmeg	Warm	Pungent	LI S St	Yang	BC QC C
Oregano	Warm	Bitter, Pungent	Liv H S K B		QC *WH*
Parsley	Warm	Bitter, Pungent, Salty	B K St	Blood	W T
Pepper, black	Hot	Pungent, Sweet	K H LI St		C D P T QC
Pepper, white	Hot	Bitter, Pungent	LI SI St		D P
Perilla	Warm	Pungent	L S		QC *WC*
Purslane	Cold	Sour	B LI Liv		H DH T
Rosemary	Warm	Pungent, Sweet	H K Liv L S	Yang	C P D *WDC*
Saffron	Neutral	Pungent, Sweet	H Liv		QC BC
Sage	Warm	Pungent, Bitter	L H K U Liv	Qi	*WH WC* H P D
Savory	Warm	Bitter, Pungent, Sweet	K L	Yang	C P QC
Tamarind	Cool	Sour, Sweet	LI SI		DH
Thyme	Warm	Bitter, Pungent	L S K B H U	Qi	P C QC *WC*
Turmeric	Warm	Bitter, Pungent	S Liv		BC QC *WDC*
Winter Savory	Warm	Pungent, Sweet, Bitter	K L	Yang	P

Medicinal Herbs & Spices

FOOD	TEMP	FLAVOUR	ROUTE	TONIFIES	REGULATES
Aconite	Hot	Pungent	H S K	Yang	C
Aloe	Cold	Bitter	Liv St LI L		H
Anemone	Cold	Bitter	H K		
Angelica root	Warm	Pungent, Bitter, Sweet	L S LI H		D C P QC *WDC*
Arnica flower	Neutral	Sweet, Bitter, Pungent	H Pe	Qi, Yin, Yang	QC
Astragalus	Warm	Sweet	S L	Qi	
Barberry	Cool	Bitter	Liv GB S St L B U		H DH QC
Bayberry bark	Warm	Pungent, Sour, Bitter	St Int Liv GB H L		QC BC P C
Bearberry leaf	Cool	Bitter, Sour	K B		DH
Bitter orange peel	Warm	Bitter, Pungent	S St Int L		QC
Bitter orange flower	Neutral	Bitter, Sweet, Pungent	Liv L St		QC DH
Black Cohosh	Cool	Pungent, Bitter, Sweet	K Liv U L	Yin, Qi	DH QC *WH*
Blackberry leaf	Cool	Sour	L B LI		P
Blackcurrant leaf	Cool	Pungent, Sweet, Sour	K Liv LI		D DH W
Blessed Thistle	Cool	Bitter	Liv		BC
Blue Cohosh	Neutral	Bitter	Liv U		QC CD *WDC*
Boneset	Cold	Bitter, Pungent	L Liv		*WH*
Borage	Cold	Sweet, Salty	Lu LI H K B	Yin	*WH*
Buchu	Hot	Pungent, Bitter, Sour	K B S	Qi	D C
Burdock root	Cool	Pungent, Bitter	L Int B K St		*WH* H D T
Burnet	Cold	Bitter, Sour	Liv LI		BC
Butterbur	Warm	Pungent, Bitter	L B K Liv U		*WC* QC T
Calamus	Neutral	Pungent	H Liv St		P D
Camphor resin	Warm	Pungent, Bitter	H L		C QC P *WC WD* BC
Catnip	Cool	Pungent, Bitter	LI L H		*WH* QC
Celandine	Warm	Pungent, Bitter	GB Liv L H		QC *WC* D DC
Cereus	Cool	Sweet, Bitter	H P U	Qi, Yang	QC
Chamomile	Cool	Bitter	LI L Liv Pe S		QC
Chaparral leaf	Cold	Bitter, Pungent, Salty	Liv K B		DH H
Chaste Tree	Neutral	Bitter, Pungent	Liv U K S		QC D
Chickweed	Cool	Sweet, Salty	L S St LI H	Yin, Blood	H
Chrysanthemum	Cold	Sweet, Bitter	L Liv	Yin	*WH* H
Cinnamon Twig	Warm	Pungent, Sweet	B H L		*WC WDC*

Medicinal Herbs & Spices *(continued)*

FOOD	TEMP	FLAVOUR	ROUTE	TONIFIES	REGULATES
Cleavers	Cool	Sour, Bitter	L K B Liv		D W DH
Coltsfoot	Warm	Pungent	L		P H
Comfrey leaf	Cool	Sweet, Bitter	L LI St B	Yin	B DH
Cornsilk	Neutral	Sweet	Liv GB B K		H D W DH
Couch Grass	Cool	Sour, Sweet	K B Liv		W DH
Cowslip Root	Neutral	Sweet, Pungent, Salty	L B		QC *WDC* P
Cramp Bark	Cool	Bitter	Liv H L B		QC BC
Damiana	Warm	Bitter, Pungent	K S Int	Yang, Qi	DC
Dandelion Root	Cold	Bitter, Sweet	K B Liv GB St Int		H W DH QC
Devil's Claw	Cool	Bitter	S St	Qi	DH
Echinacea	Cool	Pungent,Bitter, Sweet	L B		*WH* H
Elderflower	Cool	Pungent, Bitter	L B		*WH* T P H
Elecampane	Warm	Sweet, Salty, Bitter	L S Liv	Qi	P T DC
Eucalyptus	Cool	Pungent, Bitter	L LI B		P *WH* T
Eyebright	Cool	Pungent, Sour, Bitter	L		*WH* P
Feverfew	Cool	Bitter	Liv		*WH* H
Frankincense	Warm	Pungent, Bitter	H L S		BC QC *WD*
Galanga	Warm	Pungent	St		D C
Gentian	Cool	Bitter	S St Sl Liv GB	Qi, Blood	DH H
Geranium	Warm	Sweet, Pungent, Sour	S L K	Qi, Blood	W DC
Ginko leaf	Warm	Bitter	L K		BC
Ginseng (American)	Neutral	Bitter, Sweet	K L St H	Yin, Qi	
Ginseng (Chinese)	Warm	Sweet	L S	Qi	
Ginseng (Korean)	Hot	Sweet	L S	Yang, Qi	
Goldenrod	Cool	Bitter, Sour	L K		W DH
Goldenseal	Cool	Bitter	Liv GB S St L Int B U		P H DH
Hawthorn	Warm	Sweet, Sour	St Liv H	Qi	BC
Heartsease	Cool	Sour, Sweet, Bitter	L K B H	Qi	*WDC*
Hemp/cannabis seed	Neutral	Sweet	S St LI	Yin	
Hibiscus	Neutral	Sweet	B Liv		
Honeysuckle	Cold	Sweet	LI L St		H *WH* DH

Medicinal Herbs & Spices (continued)

FOOD	TEMP	FLAVOUR	ROUTE	TONIFIES	REGULATES
Hops	Cold	Bitter	H Liv Int	Yin	QC
Horny Goat Weed	Warm	Pungent, Sweet	K Liv	Yang	WDC
Horsetail	Neutral	Sweet, Bitter	L Liv		W
Jamaican Dogwood	Cold	Bitter	H Liv		
Mistletoe	Cold	Bitter, Sweet	H Liv L		QC
Jasmine flower	Warm	Pungent, Sweet	K Liv S	Yang	P C QC
Juniper	Warm	Pungent, Sweet, Sour	S K B L LI Liv		DH P QC WDC
Kava Kava	Neutral	Pungent, Bitter, Sour	K S B	Qi	D W
Kudzu	Neutral	Sweet, Bitter	S St		WH
Lady's mantle	Cold	Bitter	Liv St B LI U		H DH
Lavender	Warm	Pungent, Bitter	H Liv Int		QC D
Lemon rind	Cold	Sour, Sweet	Liv St LI H TH		H T BC QC
Licorice	Neutral	Sweet	St Int L K H	Qi	H P
Lily of the Valley	Neutral	Bitter, Sweet	H K B	Qi	BC
Limeflower	Cool	Pungent, Sweet	L Liv H		WH QC
Lobelia	Cool	Pungent	L Int H U		P QC BC
Lovage root	Warm	Bitter, Sweet, Pungent	S Liv K		W D
Marigold	Cool	Bitter	St Int		H
Marshmallow root	Cool	Sweet	L St Int B	Yin	H DH
Meadowsweet	Cool	Sweet, Bitter	St Int B		H DH W
Melissa	Cold	Bitter, Sour	H Pe TH L Liv K B		
Microalgae	Neutral	Sweet, Salty	all	Blood, Qi, Jing	
Mint	Cool	Pungent	L Liv		WH
Mistletoe	Cold	Bitter, Sweet	H Liv L		QC
Motherwort	Cool	Sour, Bitter	H U Liv	Qi	QC BC
Mugwort	Warm	Pungent, Bitter	K Liv S U	Qi	H QC
Mullein	Cool	Sweet	L St LI B	Yin	P DH
Myrrh	Warm	Pungent, Bitter	H L S Liv		QC BC P
Osha	Warm	Pungent, Bitter	L St S U		P WC

Medicinal Herbs & Spices (continued)

FOOD	TEMP	FLAVOUR	ROUTE	TONIFIES	REGULATES
Pao D'Arco	Cold	Bitter	L LI B		DH T *WH WC* P BC
Parsley seed	Neutral	Bitter, Pungent	Liv B K		QC W
Pasque flower	Neutral	Bitter, Pungent	Liv S H L LI		QC *WC WH* D
Passionflower	Neutral	Bitter	B H Liv L		QC
Pennyroyal	Warm	Pungent, Bitter	H Int U		QC *WH WC*
Perilla	Warm	Pungent	L S		QC *WC*
Pine needle	Neutral	Pungent, Bitter	L K	Yang	P
Plantain	Cold	Sweet	B SI GB Liv		H P
Pleurisy root	Cold	Bitter, Pungent	L		QC *WH* P
Poke root	Cool	Bitter	L Liv K B		P QC DH W
Pollen	Neutral	all	all	Blood, Qi, Jing	
Purslane	Cold	Sour	Liv LI B		H DH
Raspberry leaf	Neutral	Bitter, Sour	St U Int		D QC
Red Clover	Neutral	Sweet	K B L LI	Yin	D W DH T QC
Rhubarb root	Cold	Bitter, Sour	Int S Liv H		H DH QC
Rose	Cool	Sweet, Sour	S H Liv GB U		BC H QC
Rosehip	Cool	Sweet, Sour	St		H
Rue	Warm	Pungent, Bitter	K U S St H	Qi	QC C D P
Safflower	Warm	Pungent	H Liv		BC
Sandalwood	Cold	Bitter, Sweet	LI H L		DH BC QC
Sarsaparilla	Cool	Bitter, Sweet	Liv K B		DH
Sassafras	Hot	Pungent, Sweet	L S K		D W *WDC* QC
Saw Palmetto	Warm	Sweet, Sour	K B Liv S	Yang, Qi	P C
Scullcap	Cool	Bitter, Sweet	H K Liv		QC
Self Heal	Cold	Pungent, Bitter	Liv GB		H
Senna leaf	Cool	Bitter	SI U LI		H
Shepherd's Purse	Cool	Bitter, Sour	U St Liv LI		BC DH
Slippery Elm	Cool	Sweet	L St LI B	Yin	H
Solomon Seal	Cool	Sweet	L H St	Qi, Yin	
Spearmint	Cool	Pungent, Sweet	Liv L St		*WH* QC H

Medicinal Herbs & Spices *(continued)*

FOOD	TEMP	FLAVOUR	ROUTE	TONIFIES	REGULATES
Squawvine	Neutral	Sour	K Liv U		BC W
St Johns Wort	Neutral	Sour, Sweet	H K Liv		QC DH
Tansy	Cool	Bitter, Pungent	Liv S St B		QC P D DH
Tea Tree	Neutral	Sour, Sweet	L S LI Liv K		H T D P
Tormentil	Neutral	Sour, Bitter	Int		DH
Valerian	Cool	Bitter, Sweet	H Liv St Int		H
Vervain	Cool	Bitter, Pungent	L Liv K B		*WH* QC
Violet	Cool	Bitter, Pungent	Liv H		H
Wheatgrass	Neutral	Sweet, Salty	S St Liv	Qi, Blood	
White Deadnettle	Cool	Sour, Pungent	K B L U	Qi	DH B BC
White Horehound	Cool	Pungent, Bitter, Salty	L Liv S		P H *WH*
Wintergreen	Cold	Sour, Bitter, Sweet	K B Liv		*WDH* DH T W
Woad	Cold	Bitter	H St		H
Wormwood	Cool	Bitter	Liv S U		H QC
Yarrow	Cool	Bitter	L S H U	Qi	B P *WH*
Yellow Dock root	Cold	Bitter, Sour	Liv K LI	Blood	DH BC QC
Yerba Santa	Warm	Pungent, Bitter, Sour	L LI		P
Wood Sorrel	Cold	Sour	Liv K St LI		H DH

Oils & Condiments

FOOD	TEMP	FLAVOUR	ROUTE	TONIFIES	REGULATES
Olive oil	Neutral	Sweet	S Liv		
Peanut oil	Neutral	Sweet	LI L S		
Sesame oil	Cool	Sweet	St	Yin	H T
Soya oil	Warm	Pungent, Sweet	LI		BC C
Agar	Cold	Sweet, Salty	Liv L LI		H P T
Amasake	Warm	Sweet	L	Blood	BC C
Honey	Neutral	Sweet	LI L S	Yin, Qi	BC T
Kuzu	Cool	Sweet	L S St		H
Malt sugar	Warm	Sweet	L S St		BC C
Miso	Warm	Salty, Sweet	S St K	Blood	T
Molasses	Warm	Sweet	K Liv S St L	Qi, Blood	
Rice syrup	Warm	Sweet	S St		
Salt	Cold	Salty	S K LI SI St		H T
Soya sauce	Cool	Salty	S St K		H T
Sugar, brown	Warm	Sweet	Liv S St L	Qi	BC
Sugar, white	Neutral	Sweet	S St L		
Vinegar	Warm	Bitter, Sour	Liv St		QC BC C T

Beverages

FOOD	TEMP	FLAVOUR	ROUTE	TONIFIES	REGULATES
Beer	Cool	Bitter, Sweet	H S St		
Chamomile	Cool	Bitter, Sweet	LI L Liv Pe S		QC
Chrysanthemum	Cold	Bitter, Sweet	Liv L	Yin	H *WH*
Coffee	Warm	Bitter, Pungent	L Liv K St H		QC
Dandelion root	Cold	Bitter, Sweet	K B Liv GB St LI		H W DH QC
Elderflower	Cool	Bitter, Pungent	B L		*WH* T P H
Jasmine	Warm	Pungent, Sweet	K Liv S	Yang	C P QC
Lemon Balm	Cold	Bitter, Sour	H Pe L Liv K		
Limeflower	Cool	Pungent, Sweet	Liv L H		*WH* QC
Peppermint	Cool	Pungent, Sweet	Liv L S		P QC H *WH*
Raspberry leaf	Cool	Bitter, Sour	St U Int		D QC
Rosehip	Cool	Sour, Sweet	St		H
Soya milk	Neutral	Sweet	St S	Qi, Yin	H
Spirits	Hot	Pungent, Sweet, Sour	H Liv L St		QC BC C
Star Anise	Warm	Pungent, Sweet	K Liv S	Yang	QC
Tea, black	Neutral	Bitter, Sweet	H St L LI B Liv		P W QC T
Tea, green	Cool	Bitter, Sweet	H St L LI B Liv		P W QC T
Wine	Warm	Pungent, Sweet, Sour	H Liv L St		BC QC C

Common Supplements

FOOD	TEMP	FLAVOUR	ROUTE	TONIFIES	REGULATES
Algae	Cool	Salty, Sweet	all	Qi, Blood, Jing	T
Bioflavonoids	Cool		Liv		H BC
Beta-carotene	Cool		Liv		QC H T
Calcium	Cool		K	Yin	
Dangui	Warm	Sweet, Pungent	S Liv	Blood	
Folic Acid	Neutral		Liv	Blood	
Ginseng (American)	Neutral	Bitter, Sweet	K L St H	Yin, Qi	
Ginseng (Chinese)	Warm	Sweet	L S	Qi	
Ginseng (Korean)	Hot	Sweet	L S	Yang, Qi	
Iron	Cool		Liv	Yin, Blood	BC H
Pollen	Neutral	Sweet	all	Qi, Blood, Jing	
Royal Jelly	Neutral	Sweet	Liv S	Yin, Qi, Jing	
Spirulina	Cool	Salty	Liv	Blood, Yin, Jing	T
Vitamin A	Cool		Liv	Blood, Jing	H
Vitamin B complex	Warm		Liv	Blood	QC
Vitamin C	Cool		H		H
Vitamin D	Warm		K	Yang, Jing	
Vitamin E	Warm		Liv K	Blood, Yang	
Zinc	Neutral		K Liv	Blood, Jing	

Essential Oils

FOOD	TEMP	FLAVOUR	ROUTE	TONIFIES	REGULATES
Basil	Warm	Pungent, Sweet	Liv St K	Yang	C
Chamomile	Cool	Sweet	S Liv		H
Clary Sage	Cool	Pungent, Sweet	H Liv K		H
Frankincense	Cool	Pungent, Bitter	H L K		QC BC
Geranium	Neutral	Sweet	Liv K	Yin	QC
Ginger	Hot	Pungent	L S St K	Yang	D *WC* BC
Jasmine	Cool	Sweet	Liv K	Yin	H
Juniper	Warm	Pungent, Bitter	Liv K		*WDC* DC
Lavender	Cool	Pungent, Sweet	L Liv Pe		QC H *WH*
Neroli	Cool	Pungent, Sweet	H S St		D
Peppermint	Cool	Pungent	L Liv		QC *WH*
Rose	Neutral	Sweet	Liv H K	Yin	H QC BC
Sandalwood	Cool	Pungent, Bitter	L S K B		DH P
Tea Tree	Cool	Pungent, Bitter	L K		DH *WH*
Thyme	Cool	Pungent, Bitter	L K St	Qi	H P
Wintergreen	Warm	Sweet	K B		*WDC*

PART FOUR

Diagnosis

DIAGNOSIS

Diagnosis is best left to a practitioner of Chinese medicine. However, to get started, the simple checklist of signs and symptoms below will help you to establish your condition and begin the journey. As diagnosis relies on far more than simple question and answer this questionnaire is necessarily a simplification and cannot include the subtle observation of pulse, tongue, voice, emotion, appearance, movement or any of the other ingredients of a comprehensive diagnosis. So take this as a first step, see if it engages you and go see a practitioner if you want to take it further.

Each of the major patterns will present various general signs and symptoms which help us to recognise its presence. One sign or symptom is not enough to confirm a diagnosis as there can be many causes for each, but when a cluster of signs appears we are probably getting closer to seeing the pattern of disharmony.

Each general pattern may focus on one or more Organs. In this case there are some of the pattern's general signs and symptoms plus signs arising from an Organ's specific field of activity e.g. a collection of signs that includes night sweats, insomnia and flushed cheeks plus an aching lower back and low-pitch tinnitus would suggest a pattern of Kidney Yin Deficiency.

Real life is not as straightforward as this slim manual. Most people will present more than one pattern and these might even seem contradictory at first. Don't worry. This section is only a starting point, intended to stimulate your interest in Chinese medicine, not to give you indigestion or to feed any neurosis you may have about your health or about food!

PATTERNS OF DEFICIENCY

YIN DEFICIENCY

General signs and symptoms

low grade fever especially during the afternoon
feeling of heat in palms, soles and upper chest
    or face
flushed cheeks
dry throat at night
night sweats
emaciation
insomnia (shallow sleep with frequent waking)
nervousness

Signs and symptoms pointing to specific Organs

Kidney Yin Deficiency
dizziness/vertigo
low frequency ringing in the ears
hearing loss
memory loss
adrenal hyperactivity
aching lower back
deep ache in the bones (feeling "bone tired")
low sperm production
nocturnal emissions
blood in urine

Liver Yin Deficiency
disturbed sleep
irritability
dry stools
numbness in the limbs
scanty or absent menstruation
dry eyes
depression
hypertension

Stomach Yin Deficiency
no appetite
dry mouth
dry stools
thirst without desire to drink
feeling full after eating

Lung Yin Deficiency
dry or tickly throat
irritating but unproductive dry cough
blood in sputum

Heart Yin Deficiency
palpitations
feeling of restlessness
forgetfulness
intense dreaming
easily startled

YANG DEFICIENCY

General signs and symptoms

tiredness
feeling cold
cold limbs
fear of cold
feel worse in winter/better in summer
lack of thirst
desire for hot drinks
pale face
loose watery stools
frequent pale urination
lack of motivation
timidity

Signs and symptoms pointing to specific Organs

Kidney Yang Deficiency
aching lower back
cold and weak knees
weak bladder
pale, copious urine
loose watery stools
oedema in the lower body
impotence in men and infertility in women
loss of hearing

Spleen Yang Deficiency
tendency to bloat after eating
loose stools
oedema
low appetite
bloating and tiredness after eating
chilliness
cold limbs

Heart Yang Deficiency
lethargy
palpitations
shortness of breath on exertion
discomfort around the heart
depression
cold hands
profuse sweating

QI DEFICIENCY

General signs and symptoms

tiredness
reduced appetite
shortness of breath
spontaneous daytime sweating
loose stools
pale face
weak voice
slight sensitivity to cold

Signs and symptoms pointing to specific Organs

Spleen Qi Deficiency
limbs feel heavy and weak
tendency to bloat after eating
problems digesting food
tiredness after eating
loose stools
appetite low or erratic
poor concentration
food intolerances
anemia
prolapse

Stomach Qi Deficiency
tiredness in morning
lack of taste
weak limbs
loose stools
discomfort in epigastrium

Lung Qi Deficiency
weak, low voice
lack of desire to talk
weak breathing pattern
tendency to collect sputum in the lungs
shortness of breath on exertion
weak cough
tendency towards coughs and colds
tendency to daytime sweating

Kidney Qi Deficiency
frequent urination
weakness or achiness in the lower back
weakness of the skeletal structure especially at the
  knees or ankle
poor retention of urine and/or sexual fluids
chronic vaginal discharge
some shortness of breath
tendency to feel chilled
prolapse of uterus

Heart Qi Deficiency
tiredness
shortness of breath on exertion
palpitations
lethargy and a lack of spiritedness
spontaneous sweating

BLOOD DEFICIENCY

General signs and symptoms

pale and dull complexion
dizziness on standing
blurred vision or 'floaters'
dry lustreless hair
pale lips
scanty or absent menstruation
poor memory
difficulty getting to sleep
a general sense of anxiety and slight depression
tiredness

Signs and symptoms pointing to specific Organs

Liver Blood Deficiency
visual disturbance
floaters in field of vision
numbness or weakness or mild spasm in the
    muscles and tendons
weak or pale fingernails
dizziness
scanty, light or even absent menstruation

Heart Blood Deficiency
palpitations
insomnia
anxiety
intense dreaming
forgetfulness
easily startled
dizziness

ESSENCE DEFICIENCY

slow physical development
poor skeletal development
late closure of fontanelle
premature aging
greying or falling of hair
senility
poor teeth
brittle bones
general reproductive weakness

PATTERNS OF EXCESS

INTERNAL HEAT

General signs and symptoms

fever
redness
inflammation
thirst
red eyes
burning sensations
scanty, dark urination
constipation
yellow coating on tongue

INTERNAL COLD

General signs and symptoms

chilliness
desire for warm places, food and drink
abdominal pain that feels worse for pressure
lack of thirst
loose stools
abundant clear urination
white coating on the tongue
pale face
blue-tinged tongue, lips or extremities

INTERNAL DAMPNESS

General signs and symptoms

feeling of bodily heaviness
lack of appetite
feeling of congestion in or just below the chest
difficulty passing urine
sticky taste in the mouth
dirty or sticky discharges
muzzy head

Signs and symptoms pointing to specific Organs

Dampness in Spleen
full feeling in epigastrium
nausea
low appetite
loose stool
muzzy head
no taste or unpleasant sweet taste in mouth
feel tired and heavy
sticky yellow coating on tongue

Dampness and Heat in Liver and Gallbladder
fever
dark, scanty urine
fullness in and below chest
nausea, maybe vomiting
abdominal distension
inability to tolerate fats
bitter taste in mouth
jaundice
vaginal itching and/or discharge

Dampness and Heat in Large Intestine
abdominal pain
diarrhoea
smelly stools
mucus or blood in stool
burning in anus
feeling of heaviness

Phlegm in the Lungs
chronic coughing fits
pale sputum
shortness of breath
stuffy feeling in chest
worse for lying down
white coating on tongue

Phlegm and Heat in the Lungs
yellow or green phlegm
barking cough
stuffiness of chest
shortness of breath
yellow coating on tongue

Dampness and Cold in Bladder
difficult, frequent and urgent urination
pale, cloudy urination
heavy feeling in urethra

Dampness and Heat in Bladder
difficult, frequent and urgent urination
burning sensation when urinating
dark yellow, cloudy urine
blood in urine

INVASION OF WIND

General signs and symptoms

sudden onset
wandering pain and agitation mostly affecting the
upper parts of the body
aversion to wind and cold/reluctance to go
  outside
chilliness
occipital ache/ stiff neck
runny nose
sneezing

Invasion of Wind Heat

moderate fever
shivering
sneezing
cough
stuffy or runny nose with yellow mucus
swollen tonsils
sore throat
thirst
mild sweating
aversion to cold

Invasion of Wind Cold

chills
shivering
aches and pains
stiffness and little or no fever
itchy throat
sneezing
coughing
occipital headache
runny nose
no sweating
no thirst
aversion to cold

Invasion of Wind Damp

puffy, swollen eyes and face
aversion to wind
cough with watery mucus
sweating
no thirst
itchy skin and rashes which move from place
  to place
painfully swollen joints and aching muscles
symptoms are worse for humidity
general feeling of heaviness

STAGNATION OF QI

General signs and symptoms

frustration
distension of abdomen or throat
tenderness beneath ribcage
wandering distending pains
depression and irritability
volatile moods
frequent sighing
symptoms worse for stress
purplish tongue

Signs and symptoms pointing to specific Organs

Liver Qi Stagnation

frustration or inappropriate anger
tenderness and distension beneath ribcage or in
  chest
feeling of lump in the throat
lumps in groin or breast
breast tenderness before menstruation
irregular periods
menstrual pain
digestion easily disturbed by stress
belching

STAGNATION OF BLOOD

General signs and symptoms

pain which is stabbing and fixed in one location
purple lips and tongue
fixed abdominal lumps
bleeding with dark blood and a tendency towards
  blood clots
premenstrual pain

Signs and symptoms pointing to specific Organs

Liver Blood Stagnation

premenstrual pain
dark, clotted menstrual blood
abdominal lumps

Heart Blood Stagnation

palpitations
oppressive discomfort in chest
cold hands
heart pain radiating towards or along left arm

ENDNOTES

These few final notes address some of the questions most commonly asked about oriental medicine's viewpoint on food.

Raw versus Cooked

Raw food diets are popular in the West. They help to detoxify the system and in the short-term may give increased vitality. The raw food approach is one of several dietary responses to our culture's high-stress lifestyle.

From the viewpoint of oriental medicine (to which the raw food diet is foreign), the art of using raw food is knowing when to stop. Raw food is Cold and Reducing. Therefore people who are Hot and Excess will benefit more from its use. Those with weak Spleens or Deficient and Cold people will tend to be further weakened by its use. Our tolerance of raw food will also depend on where we live, hot and dry climates being preferable to cold and damp ones.

To know our tolerance of raw food, we need to know our constitution. A measure of raw foods in the diet maintains our supply of beneficial enzymes but the long-term use of raw food diets may damage the Digestive Fire.

Vegetarianism

Provided our constitution is reasonably strong a vegetarian diet can be sustained. However, the weaker we are, the more we may need to include meat in our diet. It is easy for a vegetarian to become deficient in Blood and Yang if attention is not given to eating a full range of tonifying foods. At the other end of the scale excess consumption of meat can be dampening and lead to the accumulation of toxins in the system. For most people two ounces of meat eaten three to four times per week is considered sufficient and beneficial.

Vegetarianism is perhaps best viewed as a spiritual practice. There are traditions for this within Chinese Taoism and many spiritual disciplines throughout the world. When a vegetarian diet is supported by a spiritual practice, the necessary nourishment can be obtained. Vegetarianism also forms part of some Qigong and Yogic practices and in this context may help us on our journey towards wellbeing. The overconsumption of meat also has implications for the planet which is our home.

Food Combining

The practice of food combining may be useful to people who experience digestive fermentation. The fermentation is caused by the reduced action of digestive enzymes and the increased action of bacteria. This approach to diet may be seen as supporting the Spleen's action of separating the pure from the impure and may be beneficial for stagnant conditions.

Supplements

All necessary nutrients are available in natural foods although there is some decline in available minerals even in organically grown foods. There is usually no need for supplements in a diverse diet of good quality food and their use as a substitute for eating well is questionable. However, it is sometimes helpful to use natural food-based products as a complement to good dietary practice. The important principle to bear in mind is that, whatever finds its way down our digestive tubes, the key factor will be the ability of our system to absorb it.

Coffee and Tea

Coffee stimulates the heart and, used appropriately, can be beneficial. However, it deserves special mention as it is a remarkably powerful drug whose effect is frequently underestimated. In terms of Traditional Chinese Medicine, coffee liberates our essential reserves of energy (Essence) to remarkable effect but does not replace them. Thus its effect is to deplete our storehouse of subtle energy and its consumption masks the reality of exhaustion.

Habitual use of coffee is not recommended. As always in Chinese Medicine, how much is appropriate depends on our constitution. Yang Deficient or Damp people will tolerate much more coffee than those who are Yin Deficient. Initially coffee is heating but its long-term effect seems to be cooling. Coffee enters the central energy pathway in the body, the Penetrating Vessel (Chong Mai), and can be particularly disruptive to women's reproductive cycle.

Tea is frequently used as an aid to digestion, especially when drunk weak and in small quantities, and when less coarse varieties are used. It tends to be cooling and those with cool constitutions will benefit from adding warm spices to their tea. Excessive consumption of strong black tea will weaken the Kidneys and Stomach. Both coffee and tea are diuretic and their over-use will also cause us to leak Qi through our urine.

Green tea, however, has only positive benefits. It protects the body against degenerative diseases and aids digestion. It is also effectice at gently leaching Dampness from the body and benefitting all Damp conditions including obesity.

Food Allergies

The majority of foods identified as commonly allergenic are classified as dampening in Chinese Medicine. The underlying cause normally involves Spleen weakness and a tendency towards Dampness, as well as disturbance of Liver function. Identification and regulation of aggravating foods is helpful, combined with a Damp-resolving and Spleen-strengthening diet (see earlier sections).

Food allergies may also have psychic and emotional roots which need to be addressed alongside dietary approaches.

Macrobiotics

Macrobiotics has some historical (though unacknowledged) precedent in the Taoist Cha'ang Ming diet. However, it is largely a modern adaptation of traditional Japanese peasant diet brought to the West by the pioneering spirit of George Ohsawa. Though superficially similar to traditional Chinese food energetics, there are several notable contradictions and differences in emphasis which mean that the systems do not match and each is better considered as a separate system.

From the viewpoint of Traditional Chinese Medicine, Macrobiotics appears flawed, over- emphasizing Yin and Yang classifications and not embracing the full spectrum of food energetics. Rather confusingly, Macrobiotics reverses some of the traditional definitions of Yin and Yang. According to Macrobiotics, Yin is rising and expansive and includes the sweet, sour and pungent flavours; Yang descends and contracts and includes the bitter and salty flavours. In Traditional Chinese Medicine Yin has an earthward and downward quality and includes the sour, salty and bitter flavours; Yang moves upwards and outwards and includes the sweet and pungent flavours.

It is also not common practice in Chinese Medicine to attempt to assign Yin or Yang labels to every food, except when useful. Foods are classified, as we have seen, according to temperature, flavour, route and action. The flaw in Macrobiotics is in its tendency towards rigid dogma, forcing a theory onto a reality which is too subtle and varied to fit neatly into formulae. The approach of Traditional Chinese Medicine tends to be more pragmatic, more easily assimilating inconsistencies.

Although Macrobiotics has frequently proved very successful in the treatment of severe conditions, often dramatically so, its rigid use needs to be relaxed over longer time periods.

Children

Most health problems in children result from either constitutional, emotional or dietary causes. A child's digestive system is weak and sensitive, particularly in the early stages of development. Consequently a frequent dietary cause of illness in early childhood is known as 'accumulation disorder', the accumulation of undigested food in the system causing blockage.

When the Spleen's action is blocked in this way problems may occur such as constipation, diarrhoea, breathing difficulties, cough, nasal discharge, ear congestion, abdominal pain and vomiting. The root may well lie in inappropriate feeding.

Inappropriate feeding may mean any of the following:

- Too much food overloading the system, especially when food is regularly used as a response to a child's discomfort.

- Inappropriate milk: sometimes cow's milk is too rich for babies and results in the formation of Phlegm or the discomfort of colic. In these cases sheep, goat or soya milk needs to be tried instead.

- Wholefoods and/or raw foods given too early are sometimes too much work for a young child's digestive system. It is better to start on foods that have been more broken down through their preparation.

- Poorly matched foods: just as with adults, a constitutionally Hot child needs more cooling foods and a Cold child more warming foods.

- Dampening foods: these foods are a common cause of phlegm and catarrh.

- Allergic reactions: some foods may cause behavioural problems. These are most frequently dampening foods and the most common include cow's milk, banana, gluten, citric acid (especially as concentrated fruit juice), refined sugar, tomatoes and additives.

- Microwaved food may cause abnormal changes in blood and immune systems and is best avoided. It is also unwise to warm human milk in a microwave as some of its immunity enhancing properties appear to be damaged.

Organic and local food

Where budget allows it is clearly preferable to buy organic food wherever possible. Studies have shown that organically grown foods contain more nutrients than their chemically grown counterparts. The lifeforce of organically grown foods is stronger and they are free of chemicals which can accumulate and cause harm to our system. It is also wise to buy local foods when available as they have travelled less far and will be fresher and well suited to the climate and season. By doing so we are also investing in a sustainable and healthy future for the land and community we live in.

Microwaves, Irradiation and Genetic Modification

Microwaves may be fast and efficient in terms of time and energy but from an energetic viewpoint they are seen as damaging the integrity of the food and wrecking the Qi. At a physical level the cell wall of a food is ruptured by the agitation of microwaves in a way not seen in conventional methods. At an energetic level, my experience as a practitioner is that those who regularly use microwave cookery eventually become deficient in Blood and Qi, suggesting to me that the nourishing aspect of microwaved foods has been damaged. Similarly, irradiated foods have sustained too much damage to their lifeforce.

The most alarming development in modern farming has been the spread of genetic modification. This practice has nothing to do with feeding the hungry or improving the efficiency of agriculture, and everything to do with the search for profit and the desire of a small, rich elite to dominate world food production with catstrophic results for the planet's ecology and the livelihoods of traditional farmers throughout the world. As regards the impact on human health, to modify the genetic make-up of a lifeform is to interfere with its Essence, or Jing. We do not yet know what the consequence will be for future generations. For the time being, complete avoidance seems the sensible option.

A NOTE ON SOURCES

The information on food energetics in this book represents the best achievable consensus of the views of today's practitioners of Traditional Chinese Medicine. Within the sprawling traditions of Chinese medicine there is plenty of varying and sometimes contradictory information about certain foods. Many foods eaten in the West are not known in China, so information about their properties is often more speculative, lacking the authority of millennia of experience. Steering a way through this maze has been a challenge.

Consequently, I have worked on the cautious principle of limiting the information in this book to the major properties of each food and only including foods about which there is some reasonable level of agreement. Many of the foods listed here have several other useful functions and properties. I have chosen only the most significant. Most foods, for example, can be said to somewhat tonify Qi and Blood as the manufacture of Qi and Blood provides the necessity for eating. I have only indicated those with a specific reputation as Qi and Blood tonics. More extensive descriptions of the properties of individual foods can be found in the books listed in the bibliography.

During the making of Helping Ourselves I have consulted frequently with a number of practitioners of Traditional Chinese Medicine. In particular I am grateful for the assistance of my friend Dr. Yifang Zhang who kindly translated for me from Chinese sources not available in English and whose insights have helped in the shaping of this book. Finally, the following considerations might be held in mind when considering the sources of information:

- Regional variations in climate and environment will produce variations in the quality and strength of a food's energetic properties.

- Wild foods will tend to be stronger than their domestic counterparts.

- Foods become weaker in their effect as we become used to them. Foods that are common in one culture may have a stronger effect in a culture where they are more rare.

- Hybrid and genetically engineered plants and animals will probably be weaker in their energetic effect.

BIBLIOGRAPHY

Acupuncture in the Treatment of Children, Julian Scott, Eastern Press 1991 edition
Arisal of the Clear, Bob Flaws, Blue Poppy Press 1991
Barefoot Doctor's Manual, Revolutionary Health Committee of Hunan Province, Routledge and Kegan Paul, 1978
Between Heaven and Earth, Harriet Beinfield and Efrem Korngold, Ballantine Books 1991
Bulletins of the Institute for Traditional Medicine, ITM 1992-1995
Chemistry of Herb Energetics, Christopher Hobbs, Extracted from Michael Tierra's Planetary Herbology, Lotus Press1988
Chinese Dietary Therapy, Liu Jilin & Gordon Peck, Churchill Livingstone, 1995
Chinese Foods for Longevity, Henry Lu, Sterling Publishing, 1990
Chinese Herbal Medicine, Daniel Reed, Thorsons, 1987
Chinese Medicated Diet, ed. Zhang Enqin, Publishing House of Shanghai College of Traditional Chinese Medicine, 1990
Chinese System of Food Cures, Henry Lu, Sterling Publishing, 1986
Clinical Handbook of Internal Medicine, Jane Lyttleton, University of West Sydney, 2002
Combining Western Herbs and Chinese Medicine, Jeremy Ross, Greenfields Press, 2003
Doctor's Manual of Chinese Food Cures and Western Nutrition Volumes 1 and 2, Henry Lu, Academy of Oriental Heritage, 1993 edition
Eating Your Way To Health - Dietotherapy in Traditional Chinese Medicine, Cai Jingfeng, Foreign Languages Press, Beijing, 1988
Energetics of Western Herbs Volumes 1 and 2, Peter Holmes, NatTrop Publishing, 1993 edition
Five Phases of Food, John Garvy, Wellbeing Books, 1983
Foundations of Chinese Medicine, Giovanni Maciocia, Churchill Livingstone, 1989
Handbook of Chinese Herbs, Him-che Leung, Institute of Chinese Medicine, 1996
Healing With Whole Foods, Paul Pitchford, North Atlantic Books, 1993
Herbs of Life, Lesley Tierra, The Crossing Press, 1992
Materia Medica, Dan Bensky and Andrew Gamble, Eastlands Press, 1986
Materia Medica of Essential Oils, Geoffrey Yuen, 2000
Prince Wen Hui's Cook, Bob Flaws, Paradigm Publications, 1993
Publications of Jiangsu Science and Technology Publishing House, (Yin Shi Zhi Liao Zhi Nan)
Tao of Healthy Eating, Bob Flaws, Blue Poppy Press, 1998
Tao of Nutrition, Maoshing Ni, Shrine of the Eternal Breath of Tao, 1987
Way to Good Health with Chinese Herbs, Hong-Yen Hsu, Oriental Healing Arts Institute, 1982
Yellow Emperor's Classic of Internal Medicine, translated by Ilza Veith, University of California Press, 1992

Useful addresses:

British Acupuncture Council

     63 Jeddo Road, London W12 9HQ tel: 0208 735 0400 www.acupuncture.org.uk

Register of Chinese Herbal Medicine

     P.O. Box 400, Wembley, Middlesex HA9 9NZ tel: 0208 904 1357

The Shiatsu Society

     P.O. Box 4580, Rugby, Warwickshire CV21 9EL tel: 0845 130 4560 www.shiatsusociety.org

Helping Ourselves is the first part of a trilogy of work by Daverick Leggett. It serves as a reference manual for its sequel, *Recipes for Self-Healing*, which explains in full detail how to use the foods and apply the principles outlined in *Helping Ourselves*. The companion to both these books, the wallcharts display the energetics of all the foods and herbs contained in *Helping Ourselves* in fully laminated colour wallcharts. Used together these four publications provide one of the most popular, comprehensive and accessible guides to the Chinese system of food energetics currently available.

The sequel.......

Recipes for Self-Healing

"A fabulous wealth of wisdom offered with clarity and wit"

by Daverick Leggett

Author of *Helping Ourselves*

250 original illustrations

by Katheryn Trenshaw

Paperback 342pp

ISBN 978 0 9524640 2 0 **£16.95**

One of the most important steps we can take towards self-empowerment is to take responsibility for our own nourishment. *Recipes for Self-Healing* gives us a set of tools to do this. With simplicity and elegance, this book conveys the wisdom and insights of traditional Chinese medicine and makes them both relevant and accessible to the modern day westerner.

Recipes for Self-Healing includes over a hundred exhilarating recipes using familiar foods that reflect the cosmopolitan nature of western cuisine. Its unique descriptions of each recipe's energetic actions enables readers to choose recipes perfectly suited to their own individual needs. Above all the author emphasises dissolving concepts of good and bad foods, the importance of pleasure and listening to the wisdom of the body.

'Recipes for Self-Healing has wonderful accessible information for the intellect, tasty delicious food for the body and wit and levity for the spirit – the complete mind, body, spirit experience.'

Jane Sen, author of *The Healing Foods Cookbook*

'These recipes are the practical application in the modern world of a 5,000 year old medical tradition. In our increasingly frantic world such wisdoms are greatly needed. This book will be of great benefit to everyone interested in..... developing a healthy way of living.'

Dr. Stephen Gascoigne, doctor, acupuncturist and herbalist

'Recipes for Self-Healing has inspired me to see diet in a totally new way, and has given me the tools necessary to truly use food as medicine. This is a great gift.'

Sandra Hill, author of *Reclaiming the Wisdom of the Body*

The Energetics of Food & The Energetics of Herbs

"A masterly condensation of information"

by Daverick Leggett

These full colour wallcharts are the ideal companion to both *Recipes for Self-Healing* and *Helping Ourselves*. Attractively designed, fully laminated and easy to use, they enable you to find at a glance the energetic properties of about 300 common foods and 150 herbs. For anyone wishing to apply the principles of food energetics in their own kitchen, The Energetics of Food and The Energetics of Herbs are the perfect companions.

ISBN 978 0 9524640 1 2 & 978 0 9524640 3 9 **£7.50**

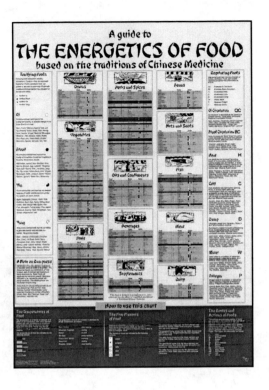

Qi Nutrition DVD

by Daverick Leggett

Qi Nutrition is a simple, clear guide to nutrition seen through the lens of Chinese medicine. It provides a thorough grounding in the basic principles, offers practical advice and concludes by putting principles into action in the kitchen with three lively and unusual recipes.

115 minutes, two discs

DVD - region free

ISBN 978 0 9524640 6 8 **£25**

All titles may be ordered by credit/debit card through our secure website

www.meridianpress.net

Meridian Press publications are distributed in:
UK by **Meridian Press**, P.O.Box 3, Totnes TQ9 5WJ tel: 0845 456 1852 email post@meridianpress.net
North America by **Redwing Books**, 202 Bendix Drive,Taos NM 87571 tel: 505 758 7758 fax: 505 758 7768
www.redwingbooks.com
Australasia by **China Books**, 234 Swanston Street, Melbourne, Victoria 3000 tel: 03 9663 8822 fax: 03 9663 8821
Also available in German as **"Selbstheilung durch Ernahrung"** ISBN 3-442-33727-5 Goldmann Arkana

ABOUT THE AUTHOR

Daverick Leggett began his working life as a farmer and gardener, then as a school teacher. He first entered the world of oriental medicine as a shiatsu practitioner. Since the early 1990's he has been working as a Qigong teacher and pursuing his interest in nutrition through private consultations and teaching. Daverick teaches both Qigong and nutrition throughout the UK and internationally.

The titles of his two books (Helping Ourselves and Recipes for Self-Healing) contain the essential intent of his work: finding ways of helping people to help themselves to deeper health and more vibrant living. Daverick lives with his son in Dartington, Devon.

Meridian Press
P.O. Box 3
Totnes
Devon TQ9 5WJ
England

Tel & Fax: 0845 456 1852
post@meridianpress.net
www.meridianpress.net

NOTES

CPSIA information can be obtained
at www.ICGtesting.com
Printed in the USA
FSOW02n1155130716
22704FS